THE YEAR-ROUND BOOK OF SERMON IDEAS, STORIES AND QUOTES

STAN TOLER

and

ELMER TOWNS

Gospel Light

Gospel Light is an evangelical Christian publisher dedicated to serving the local church. We believe God's vision for Gospel Light is to provide church leaders with biblical, user-friendly materials that will help them evangelize, disciple and minister to children, youth, adults and families.

We hope this Gospel Light resource will help you discover biblical truth for your own life and help you minister to your church and community. God bless you in your work.

For a free catalog of resources from Gospel Light please contact your Christian supplier or call 1-800-4-GOSPEL.

PUBLISHING STAFF
William T. Greig, Publisher
Dr. Elmer L. Towns, Senior Consulting Publisher
Pam Weston, Editor
Patti Pennington Virtue, Associate Editor
Christi Goeser, Editorial Assistant
Kyle Duncan, Associate Publisher
Bayard Taylor, M.Div., Senior Editor, Biblical and Theological Issues
Dr. Gary S. Greig, Senior Advisor, Biblical and Theological Issues
Kevin Parks, Cover Designer
Rosanne Richardson, Assistant Cover Designer
Debi Thayer, Designer

ISBN 0-8307-2572-5
© 2001 Gospel Light
All rights reserved.
Printed in the U.S.A.

More Holy Humor jokes and antecdotes are taken from the best of *The Joyful Noiseletter*, newsletter of the Fellowship of Merry Christians, P. O. Box 895, Portage, MI 49081-0895.

Any omission of credits is unintentional. The publisher requests documentation for future printings.

All Scripture quotations, unless otherwise indicated, are taken from the *Holy Bible, New International Version*®. Copyright © 1973, 1978, 1984 by International Bible Society. Used by permission of Zondervan Publishing House. All rights reserved.

Other versions used are:
THE MESSAGE—Scripture taken from *THE MESSAGE.* Copyright © by Eugene H. Peterson, 1993, 1994, 1995. Used by permission of NavPress Publishing Group.

RSV—From the *Revised Standard Version* of the Bible, copyright 1946, 1952 and 1971 by the Division of Christian Education of the National Council of Churches of Christ in the U.S.A. Used by permission.

How to Make Clean Copies
from this Book

You may make copies of portions of this book with a clean conscience if:
*   you (or someone in your organization) are the original purchaser;
*   you are using the copies you make for a noncommercial purpose (such as teaching or promoting your ministry) within your church or organization;
*   you follow the instructions provided in this book.

However, it is ILLEGAL for you to make copies if:
*   you are using the material to promote, advertise or sell a product or service other than for ministry fund-raising;
*   you are using the material in or on a product for sale;
*   you or your organization are **not** the original purchaser of this book.

By following these guidelines you help us keep our products affordable.
Thank you,
Gospel Light

ENDORSEMENTS

Stan Toler and Elmer Towns are two of the most creative preachers/pastors/authors/thinkers/leaders I know. Their writings are a literal avalanche of practical "how tos" for pastors and church leaders. Each book they have written helps us all to become more effectual in Kingdom expansion. And now here comes another extremely useful and badly needed tool—helps for us when preaching. Whether novices or seasoned communicators, we all have one thing in common: We look for better ways to convey the spectacular gospel of Christ. Not only does this book promise to do that—it delivers!

Dr. Jim Garlow
Senior Pastor
Skyline Wesleyan Church

This book is exactly what we as pastors need—tips and helps for those special Sundays of the year. The authors don't do our work for us, but they help us do our work. I'm going to be using it often for illustrations and ideas for that special Sunday.

Dr. Erwin W. Lutzer
Senior Pastor
The Moody Church

I am thankful for any help I can get in my sermons! Fortunately, Stan Toler has given a book which will be a help to us all. He is a fine young Nazarene pastor. What an encouragement his book will be to you.

Dr. Jerry Vines
Senior Pastor
First Baptist Church

As pastor of the same church for 15 years, my sermon tank for special days and events often runs low. No more! *The Year-Round Book of Sermon Ideas, Stories and Quotes* is a much needed fuel for my preaching tank. This book is a refreshing asset to any pastor or church leader. It is fresh, practical, biblical, easy-to-use, relevant, transferable and comprehensive. It provides a plethora of useful quotes, illustrations and outlines. I will use it again and again. Thanks to Stan Toler and Elmer Towns for your contribution to my ministry. Those who listen to me week after week should thank you as well.

Dr. David Earley
Senior Pastor
New Life Community Baptist Church

Stan Toler is a pastor's best friend. I have seen this quality displayed in the conferences he leads, the church he pastors, and the way he gets involved in helping churches and pastors right here in Oklahoma City. Stan is a gifted and godly Christian leader and a true friend. Teamed with Elmer Towns, we have the benefit of two of our country's finest leaders. It is only natural that any pastor would want to learn from their vast experience and success. They provide us with yet another opportunity in this latest writing, *The Year-Round Book of Sermon Ideas, Stories and Quotes*. I have read it cover to cover and it has become one of my primary sermon planning resources. This is a must read for every pastor.

> Rev. Marty Grubbs
> Pastor
> Crossings Community Church

Everyone appreciates a good illustration. The right illustration at the right time is half the battle for many preachers. I have been involved in the preaching ministry for over 40 years and I have found that a message normally requires three or four illustrations. *The Year-Round Book of Sermon Ideas, Stories and Quotes* will be invaluable to busy pastors . . . you cannot afford not to have this book.

> Dr. Orville Hagan
> General Director, Evangelism and
> Home Missions
> Church of God

This new book by Stan Toler and Elmer Towns is a must for all pastors who desire to communicate more effectively. It is a reservoir of helpful ideas, illustrations and outlines. I highly recommend this very practical resource.

> Dr. Doug Carter
> Vice President
> EQUIP Foundation

Stan Toler and Elmer Towns offer a great compilation for the busy pastor—or speaker—seeking hard-to-find ideas for important addresses. This collection is a must for every speaker.

> Dr. Alton Loveless
> General Director
> Randall House Publications

Stan Toler and Elmer Towns continue to capture the heart of the gospel while having a strong desire to assist the local pastor to be better prepared for preaching. Their helpfulness creates health and their creativity encourages joyful preaching.

> Dr. Jim Dunn
> Senior Pastor
> First Baptist Church

EVERY PAGE
IN THIS BOOK
IS REPRODUCIBLE!*

- Hand out copies as instructions to leaders, photocopy sermon outlines or tuck-ins for quick reference, duplicate easy-to-use litanies that you can use over and over again.
- Reproducible clip art is provided throughout the book for advertising in your church bulletin, posters, etc.

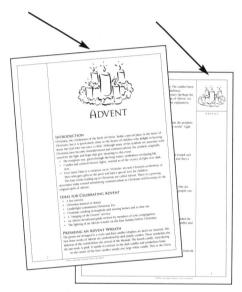

- The Scripture reference index will help guide you to the passage you're looking for.
- There's a topical index for ease in finding just the story, quote, sermon outline or idea to help you deliver your message.

CONTENTS

SPECIAL THANKS

Special thanks to Bill Greig III, Kyle Duncan, Deloris Leonard, Linda Elliott, Renee Grooms, Derl Keefer, Jerry Brecheisen, Arianna Eckart and Christy Lipscomb: You have made this project so much easier!

FOREWORD

For over 30 years I have looked for new and innovative ways to share God's Word and guidance with others. From my days as a pastor in a small rural church to my current call to speak to thousands on leadership, I have used countless illustrations to communicate with and relate to the audience. I started many years ago collecting quotes and stories, but what a treasure it would have been to start with a resource such as *The Year-Round Book of Sermon Ideas, Stories and Quotes.*

Both Stan Toler and Elmer Towns have played important roles in my ministry, and they continue to bless people with their insight and style. Stan Toler became a wonderful friend as we worked together early in my ministry. Today he pastors Trinity Church of the Nazarene in Oklahoma City and continues to work with me as the model church instructor for the INJOY Group. Within this book he shares some of the humorous illustrations that have set him apart as a speaker and best-selling author.

Elmer Towns influenced my early ministry as a pastor with his best-selling books on Sunday School, first published over 30 years ago. I enjoy his insight, practical approach and powerful presentation. He, along with Stan, leads the Teaching to Influence Lives conferences sponsored by The INJOY Group. Throughout this book, Elmer shares his illustrations from years of research and his experiences as a pastor and teacher.

As pastors we look to the Holy Spirit for guidance—in our lives and in our ministries. When preparing sermons, we first look to God and His Word. In relating His Word to our congregations, we often need common examples and shared experiences. Jesus gave us a wonderful model to follow as He used parables and examples during His ministry on Earth. We first must have an understanding of the Scriptures to speak with authority, and only then can we begin to prepare to relate them through stories and illustrations.

The Year-Round Book of Sermon Ideas, Stories and Quotes will assist you in bringing life to your lessons. Stan and Elmer have done a tremendous job of collecting illustrations that every pastor can use to relate God's Word. I know this book can make a difference in your life and the lives of those you lead.

Dr. John C. Maxwell

Founder, The INJOY Group

INTRODUCTION

People journey toward truth by taking the familiar route. Jesus clearly taught that principle by His own ministry. "Without using a parable . . ." (see Mark 4:34).

You hold in your hand a valuable tool that will expand your ministry and help you communicate to the people in your church. You have dozens and dozens of illustrations and stories for every event in your church year. Some stories are funny to motivate your church to laughter, some illustrations will bring tears, while others are designed to marshal the troops to action.

People will remember stories when they forget the preacher's sermon or the Sunday School teacher's lesson. When Jesus wanted to get across His message, He used parables, which were stories that helped the listeners understand and apply the message.

You probably have heard a lot of stories, but you forget them. You never seem to have the right story for the right occasion. This book will help you because we've arranged them around *The Year-Round Church Event Book*.

This book will help because of the convenient clip-art approach, allowing you to paste items in your bulletins or, in the case of some illustrations, copy the entire page and slip it into the church bulletin for special Sundays, rallies, banquets or dedication services.

We have been gathering these illustrations throughout our ministry in large and small churches. There is no claim for complete originality. The stories, sermons and dedications have blessed our congregations. We share them with you to bless your church.

> You are loved,
> Elmer Towns and Stan Toler

Section One

~

RITUAL
CELEBRATIONS
AND SERVICES

ADVENT

HISTORY OF ADVENT

But Mary treasured up all these things and pondered them in her heart.
Luke 2:19

The sacred night of the Savior's birth was first a sacred reflection in the heart of His mother. The truest Christmas observance is sacred not secular. It's not about activities and shopping lists; it's all about attitude and eternal life. The hope of every heart was born in an obscure village to an obedient but obscure young woman. The word she received from heaven's messenger began a process of reflection that culminated in the birth of the Messiah.

Advent is the season preceding Christmas that anticipates Christ's birth. This season begins on the Sunday nearest November 30, which is known as St. Andrew's Day.[1] It concludes on Christmas Eve. Today, Advent marks the beginning of the ecclesiastical year.[2]

In the 500s, Advent was a time of penitence that lasted six weeks. Later the Advent season was reduced to four weeks.[3] It has continued since that time to be a somber yet joyful time of preparation for the arrival of Jesus on Earth. Churches commonly depict this joyful reverence by lighting an Advent candle for each new week of Advent.

While Advent continues to be a time of remembering the events leading up to the incarnation, many worshipers also recognize another symbolic meaning. We are in a period of time awaiting the second arrival of Christ. He has promised to someday return to Earth again, this time as the mighty conqueror. Until He returns, we are in a season of perpetual Advent. As we wait for His return, we can celebrate Jesus' first arrival. These four sacred weeks provide a beautiful time for worshipers to reflect on Christ's gracious gift of Himself to us.

SERMON SKETCHES

ADVENT SUNDAY

THE REASON FOR THE SEASON —STAN TOLER

MAIN TEXT: JOHN 1:1-16

1. Jesus came to identify with humankind.

   He was in the world, and though the world was made through him, the world did not recognize him (v. 10).

2. Jesus came to give hope to discouraged people.

   Yet to all who received him, to those who believed in his name, he gave the right to become children of God (v. 12).

3. Jesus came to give life a new outlook.

   From the fullness of his grace we have all received one blessing after another (v. 16).

4. Jesus came to give truth a new perspective.

   The Word became flesh and made his dwelling among us. We have seen his glory, the glory of the One and Only, who came from the Father, full of grace and truth (v. 14).

   For God so loved the world that he gave his one and only Son, that whoever believes in him shall not perish but have eternal life (John 3:16).

SERMON
SKETCHES

THE SACRIFICE OF CHRISTMAS —JERRY BRECHEISEN

MAIN TEXT: PHILIPPIANS 2:5-11

1. The giver of life became the gift of life.

    Who, being in very nature God, did not consider equality with God something to be grasped (v. 6).

2. The Prince of Peace became a pauper.

    But made himself nothing, taking the very nature of a servant, being made in human likeness (v. 7).

3. The sinless One died a sinner's death.

    And being found in appearance as a man, he humbled himself and became obedient to death—even death on a cross! (v. 8).

ADVENT CALL TO WORSHIP

On this first Sunday of Advent,
Let us look backward to Bethlehem in gratitude for the Christ who was.
Let us look forward to the trumpet call in expectation of the Christ who
    is to come.
Let us look inward to the presence of the Spirit in assurance of the Christ
    who is here.
As we come together to worship,
Let us respond to the exhortation of John the Baptist;
Let us prepare the way of the Lord.
Let us prepare His way in our city.
Let us prepare His way in the sanctuary.
Let us prepare His way in our homes.
Let us prepare His way in our lives.
Come, let us prepare the way of the Lord. —Author unknown

PRAYERS

ADVENT INVOCATION

As we enter this Advent season,
May we find it to be beautiful, a time of glowing lights and bright colors,
May we find it to be happy, a time of smiles and bright faces.
May we find it to be heartwarming, a time of inspiration and encouragement.
May we find it to be challenging, a time of rededication and renewal.
And may this experience of Advent begin this very moment. —Author unknown

ADVENT PRAYER

Grant, Almighty God, that looking forward in faith to the feast of our Lord's birth, we may feel all the happiness our Savior brings, and celebrate His coming with unfailing joy. —Mark Connolly, "Advent," *Spirituality for Today.* http://www.spirituality.org/issue04/page ll html (accessed November 1995).

CHRISTMAS PRAYER OF CONFESSION

If we have been superficial in our Christmas preparations,
  Lord of Christmas, forgive us.
If we have sung the musical notes with our voices, but not with our hearts,
  Lord of Christmas, forgive us.
If we have invested money in gifts, but have not invested ourselves in love,
  Lord of Christmas, forgive us.
If we have made beautiful our homes, but have not enhanced our lives,
  Lord of Christmas, forgive us.
If we have rejoiced with family and friends, but have neglected the poor and destitute,
  Lord of Christmas, forgive us. —Author unknown

QUOTES

QUOTES

The feet of the humblest may walk in the fields
Where the feet of the holiest have trod.
This is the marvel to mortals revealed,
When the silvery trumpets of Christmas have pealed,
That mankind are the children of God. —Phillips Brooks

KEEP CHRISTMAS WITHIN

Then let every heart keep Christmas within:
Christ's pity for sorrow,
Christ's hatred for sin,
Christ's care for the weakest,
Christ's courage for right.
Everywhere, everywhere,
Christmas tonight. —Phillips Brooks

THE CHRISTMAS LIST

I had the nicest Christmas list, the longest one in town,
Till Father looked at it and said, "You'll have to cut it down."
I knew that what he said was true, beyond the faintest doubt,
But was amazed to hear Him say, "You've left your best Friend out."
And so I scanned my list again, and said, "That's just not true!"
But Father said, "His name's not there, the Friend who died for you."
And then I clearly understood—'twas Jesus that He meant:
For Him who should come first of all, I hadn't planned a cent. —Author unknown

'TWAS THE NIGHT BEFORE

'Twas the night before Christmas and all through the house,
Not a creature was stirring 'cept Dad and his spouse.
Their faces were haggard, all wrinkled with care.
They looked at each other and sighed with despair.
Could they both be enjoying the presents they got?
From the look on their faces, we knew they were not.
It was simple to us what was causing their ills.
They were figuring out how to pay all the bills. —Author unknown

Everybody'd be happier this Christmas if we'd just cut the cost and revive the reverence. —Oren Arnold, "The Head Man," *Bluebook* (December 1955), p. 41.

It must be said that we can have joy, and therefore will have it, only as we give it to others. —Karl Barth

He who has not Christmas in his heart will never find it under a tree. —Roy L. Smith, quoted in *The Vance Havner Quote Book*, comp. Dennis J. Hester (Grand Rapids, MI: Baker Book House, 1986), p. 39.

Give what you have. To someone, it may be better than you dare to think. —Henry Wadsworth Longfellow

When the message was first given it was given not to religious priests, but to shepherds, men of action who were fulfilling their ordinary duties. This put the message into the stream of ordinary life. —E. Stanley Jones

'Tho Christ a thousand times in Bethlehem be born, if He's not born in thee, thy soul is still forlorn. —Angelus Silesisies, quoted in *The Vance Havner Quote Book*, comp. Dennis J. Hester (Grand Rapids, MI: Baker Book House, 1986), p. 79.

That there was no room in the inn was symbolic of what was to happen to Jesus. The only place there was room for Him was on the Cross. —William Barclay

19

A TRUE CELEBRATION OF ADVENT

No matter how commercial Advent and Christmas become, we are still in control of our own lives. It can be made sacred and spiritual if we make the preparations for Christmas a true celebration of Advent—a time of reflection on the beautiful mystery of the birth of Christ. —Mark Connolly, "Advent," *Spirituality for Today*. http://www.spirituality.org/issue04/page 11.html (accessed November 1995).

THE SOUND OF THE CHRISTMAS BELLS

There are sounds in the sky when the year grows old,
And the winds of the winter blow—
When night and the moon are clear and cold,
And the stars shine in the snow,
Or wild is the blast and the bitter sleet
That bleats on the window pane;
But blest on the frost hills are the feet
Of the Christmas time again!
Chiming sweet when the night winds swells,
Blest is the sound of the Christmas bells! —Author unknown

THAT'S LOVE

It's a cruel and ugly world. It always has been. So what does that have to do with Christmas? A lot. It tells you where to look for love—in a stinky food trough where a tiny infant squirms on stale hay 2,000 years ago. Entombed within the tender flesh of that tiny baby was the God of the universe, making the ultimate sacrifice to reconcile men to Himself. That's love. And that's the source of a merry Christmas. —Chuck Swindoll, *Improving Your Serve* (Nashville, TN: Word Publishing, 1981), pp. 112, 113.

In the body of that little child, in the incarnate Son of God, your flesh, all your distress, anxiety, temptation, all your sin, is borne, forgiven, and healed. —Dietrich Bonhoffer

GLAD ABOUT GOD

The coming of Jesus Christ into the world brought the peace of God into the hearts of men—and with peace came joy. As Joseph Fort Newton wrote, "For the first time man was glad about God." —John Middlekauff, quoted in *Speaker's Illustrations for Special Days*, ed. Charles L. Wallis (New York: Abingdon Press, 1956), p. 36.

Christ is the coming of God—revealed to us in the persuasive terms of personal life and loving will. —Rufus M. Jones, quoted in *Speaker's Illustrations for Special Days*, ed. Charles L. Wallis (Grand Rapids, MI: Baker Book House, 1956), p. 29.

ORIGIN OF SOME CHRISTMAS TRADITIONS

- The Christmas tree began as a German tradition as early as A.D. 700 and moved to England and America through immigrants.
- The first manufactured Christmas tree ornament was sold at Woolworth's in 1880. Martin Luther is credited with first decorating trees with candles in the sixteenth century. Calvin Coolidge ceremoniously lit the first outdoor tree at the White House in 1923.
- Mistletoe has been used as a decoration for thousands of years, but because of its association with pagan rituals, the Church forbade its use in any form, suggesting holly as a substitute. The pointed leaves of the holly symbolize the thorns on Christ's crown and the red berries, the drops of His blood.
- Christmas cards started in London in 1843 and in America in 1848. Today, about two billion Christmas cards are exchanged each year in the United States. —Marshall Brain, "How Christmas Works," *How Stuff Works.* http://www.howstuffworks.com (no access date).

QUOTES

21

ILLUSTRATIONS

ILLUSTRATIONS

AN UNFORGETTABLE CHRISTMAS

Christmas Day 1961 will always be a memorable day for the Toler family. Winter had been long and hard with lots of snow and cold weather. Times were tough! Dad was laid off from construction work, our food supply dwindled to nothing, and we closed off most of the house due to our inability to afford high utility bills.

On Christmas Eve, Mom noted we would have no food on Christmas Day. She suggested that we accept a handout from the government Commodity Department. So Dad loaded Terry and me into his old Plymouth and we headed downtown. That evening we stood in line with others for what seemed like hours, waiting on the government handouts—cheese, dried milk, flour and dried eggs.

Finally, Dad could stand it no longer. "We're going home, boys," he said. "God will provide!" We cried but completely trusted Dad's faith in God.

That night, we popped popcorn and opened the gifts we had ordered with Mom's Top Value Trading Stamps, saved for Christmas presents. Terry ordered a transistor radio, I ordered a Brownie Kodak camera, and Mark got a baby toy. We were so grateful to have anything!

Everyone slept well under Grandma's handmade quilts that night. We were just happy to be together as a family.

On Christmas Day morning, December 25, 1961, we were startled by a loud knock and Merry Christmas greetings from people who attended our church. They arrived with gifts, clothing and a 30-day supply of food. Since that day, I have always believed that God will provide and that whenever there is a need, He has a prearranged supply to meet the need through His people. —Stan Toler

THE CHRISTMAS GIFT

Frank Meade quotes from the *First Baptist Church Bulletin* from Syracuse, New York: "There was a gift for each of us under the tree of life 2,000 years ago by Him whose birthday we celebrate today. The gift was withheld from no man. Some have left the packages unclaimed. Some have accepted the gift and carried it around, but have failed to remove the wrappings and to look inside to discover hidden splendor. The packages are all alike. In each is a scroll on which is written, "All that the Father has is yours. Take and live!" —Frank Meade, comp., *12,000 Religious Quotations* (Grand Rapids, MI: Baker Book House, 1989), p. 70.

22

THE CHRISTMAS MESSAGE

On Christmas Eve, the headmaster of a children's home was preparing his Christmas message. A dorm mother knocked on the door and explained that one of the children was upset because he didn't get to go home for Christmas.

Following her to the boy's room, the headmaster discovered the troubled boy under his bed. Standing next to the bed, he tried to converse with him but there was no response.

Finally, he dropped to his knees and lifted the bed spread. Tear-stained eyes looked out. Instead of forcefully pulling the boy out, he dropped to the floor, crawled under the bed and held out his hand.

Finally, the boy placed his tiny hand into the hand of the headmaster.

The headmaster had his Christmas message. God stooped to the earth and gave us Jesus. In our fear, loneliness and sin, He crawled in beside us and held out His hand. —Henry Carter, quoted in *Guideposts* (1978), n.p.

I'VE WANTED ONE OF THESE

After ripping into a Christmas present, a three-year-old girl picked up the toy and said, "Ooohhh, I've wanted one of these ever since I was a little girl."

The marvelous thing about the joy of Christmas is that we didn't know we wanted it until it came. And the minute we first beheld God's glory wrapped in swaddling clothes, we knew it was what we had always wanted; what we had always needed. It fills us with joy. —Michael Duduit, ed., *The Abingdon Preaching Annual 1997* (Nashville, TN: Abingdon Press, 1996), p. 16.

GREATER THAN A WALK ON THE MOON

Noted preacher Charles L. Allen said that he lived around the block from one of the astronauts who walked on the moon. Commenting on the thrill of living near one who had a part in that historic event, Allen added, "The greatest event in human history was not when a human being walked on the moon. The greatest event in human history was when God became a man." —Dennis J. Hester, comp., *The Vance Havner Quote Book* (Grand Rapids, MI: Baker Book House, 1986), p. 88.

23

ILLUSTRATIONS

CHRISTMAS IN A PRISONER OF WAR CAMP

Rep. John McCain, (R., Arizona) wrote of his last Christmas as a prisoner of war in North Vietnam. The previous Christmas was marked by his captor's cruelty, who punished McCain and the other prisoners for celebrating the birth of Christ.

Meeting this time with fear and trembling, they sang hymns and carols. "Suddenly we were 2,000 years and half a world away in a village called Bethlehem. And neither war, nor torture, nor imprisonment, nor the centuries themselves had dimmed the hope born on that silent night so long ago. In a place designed to turn men into animals, we clung to one another, sharing what comfort we had." He continues, "The Vietnamese guards did not disturb us. But as I looked up at the barred windows, I wished they had been looking in. I *wanted* them to see us—faithful, joyful, and yes, triumphant." —John R. McCain, "Joyful and Triumphant," *Reader's Digest* (December 1984), p. 84.

WHAT MAKES CHRISTMAS PERFECT?

As a little girl, I thought Christmas was perfect the year I received my shiny green and silver Western Flyer bicycle. I had slipped out of bed on Christmas Eve night to sneak a peek at gifts under the tree. However, I was halted at the door by an eerie yet wonderful gleam from the living room. Something was reflecting the moonlight from the window. The next morning, I discovered my beautiful bike.

As a young teen, I thought the perfect Christmas was spent at my grandparents' home on Christmas Day. Nanny always made roast turkey with two kinds of dressing, two other meats and a multitude of fancy delicacies. But now my grandparents are gone. The old farmhouse has been sold. The Christmases at that country farmhouse seemed perfect, but now they are only treasured memories.

As a young adult, I remember the adventure of my first Christmas with my husband, Stan, and his family. We were engaged to be married; life was wonderful. We were in love. It was the perfect Christmas! But, even so, it meant being away from my parents for the first time at Christmas. I remember Mother cried when I gave her a very crude, little clay pitcher I had made in a college art class. I realize now, it couldn't have been the perfect Christmas, if separation and sadness were a part of it.

Now I think I have a better understanding of what makes the perfect Christmas. It doesn't matter about age, occupation or social position. All that really counts is the relationship I have with Jesus Christ.

For the perfect Christmas, we must experience Jesus as our Lord and Savior.
—Linda Toler

24

THE STAR IN THE WINDOW

Christmas Eve sometime during World War II a little boy and his father were driving home from shopping at the grocery store in town. They drove past rows of houses with their Christmas trees and decorations lighting the windows. In several of the windows the boy noticed a star. He inquired of his father, "Daddy, why do some of the people have a star in the window?" His father said that the star meant that the family had a son in the war. As they passed the last house out of town on their way home, there was a large open space. Suddenly the little boy caught sight of the evening star in the sky. "Look Daddy, God must have a son in the war too! He's got a star in His window." —James Hewett, ed., *Ilustrations Unlimited* (Wheaton, IL: Tyndale House Publishers, 1988), p. 84.

THE IMAGE OF GOD

A famous fresco in Rome, called "The Aurora," was painted on the ceiling of a palace! Looking up to see it, you can become dizzy and stiff-necked as the figures become indistinct. After several complaints, the palace owner placed a mirror near the floor. The reflection of the picture becomes clearer and you can sit for hours and contemplate its beauty.

Frank Fairchild observed, "Jesus Christ does precisely that for us when we try to get some notion of God. He is the mirror of Deity—the express image of God's person. In Him, God becomes visible and intelligible to us. We cannot, by any amount of searching, find God. The more we try, the more we are bewildered. Then Jesus Christ appears. He is God stooping down to our level, and He enables our feeble thoughts to get some real hold on God Himself." —Walter Knight, *Knight's Master of New Illustrations* (Grand Rapids, MI: Eerdmans Publishing Company, 1956), p. 78.

ILLUSTRATIONS

25

ILLUSTRATIONS

THE FORGIVENESS GIFT

It was the perfect Christmas Eve. Dad was home early. After supper, he built a fire in the fireplace, while Mother made up a big tray of goodies. The kids jumped and ran and shouted in their excitement. Finally when their older sister arrived with her husband, the family gathered together in the den around the Christmas tree. They sang Christmas carols, exchanged gifts with one another, snacked on all the goodies, then ended the evening by walking through the snow to the annual candlelight service. A Christmas Eve to remember.

Christmas Eve. We plan for it and look forward to it. It's a time of pleasant memories and nostalgia.

This may not be the case in every home. For some families, Christmas Eve turns out to be a great battlefield with mines and torpedoes mixed. There is no peace on Earth, much less in the home. Our expectations often run high and our disappointments deep. The gift hoped for is the gift never given. The son who said he would be there—isn't. The sister who never has a kind word for anyone started one of her many tirades.

If that's your experience today, then even though it may be difficult, wrap up one more gift and give it away—the gift of forgiveness. It may be the most important, and most beautiful, gift you will ever give to another person. —*Daylight Devotional Bible New International Version* (Grand Rapids, MI: Zondervan Publishing House, 1988), p. 1263.

WHERE IS JESUS' PRESENT?

Little Linda was allowed to pass out the Christmas gifts the Christmas Eve she learned to read. According to family custom, the one who distributed the presents would be allowed to open the first gift. After all the presents were distributed with care, Linda kept looking around among the branches. Her father asked, "Honey, what are you looking for?"

The little girl replied, "I thought Christmas was Jesus' birthday and I was just wondering where His present is. I guess everyone forgot Him. Did they, Daddy?" —Eleanor Doan, comp., *The Speaker's Sourcebook* (Grand Rapids, MI: Zondervan Publishing House, 1960), p. 58.

CHRISTMAS PREACHER

A four-year-old recited her version of a holiday favorite, "'Twas the night before Christmas and all through the house, not a *preacher* was stirring, not even a mouse." —Perry Greene

26

THE CLEAN WISE MEN

The five-year-old broke into the family Christmas carol singing, "I'm glad those shepherds were nuts about being clean!"

"Why do you say that?" Dad asked.

The boy replied, "The song says the shepherds washed their socks by night."
—Author unknown

SYNCHRONIZED SHOPPING

A family went Christmas shopping at the mall. Outside the entrance, Dad assembled Mom and the kids.

"We'll meet back here in two hours," Dad announced, "so let's synchronize our watches."

Mom tapped Dad on the shoulder. "I think we ought to synchronize our credit cards too." —Author unknown

POLITICALLY CORRECT GREETING

Best wishes for an environmentally conscious, socially responsible, low stress, non-addictive, gender neutral, winter solstice holiday, practiced with the most joyous traditions of the religious persuasion of your choice, but with respect for the religious persuasion of others who choose to practice their own religion as well as those who choose not to practice a religion at all; plus, a fiscally successful, personally fulfilling, and medically uncomplicated recognition of the generally accepted calendar year, but not without due respect for the calendars of choice of the other cultures whose contributions have helped make our society great, without regard to age, race, creed, color, religion, national origin, disability, political affiliation or sexual orientation. —Author unknown

LOOK INSIDE

The little neighbor boy got a trumpet for Christmas. His loud playing bothered the elderly gentleman next door, until one day he stopped the boy outside. "What do you call that beautiful instrument I hear you playing?"

"It's a trumpet," the boy replied.

"What's inside that thing that makes it sound so lovely?"

"I don't know," the boy answered.

The neighbor pulled out a screwdriver and a set of pliers, "Here, take these and look inside." —Author unknown

IS SANTA CLAUS REAL?

Little five-year-old Victoria seemed more subdued than normal as her father drove her to school. Her father, Fred, said, "You seem deep in thought. What are you thinking about?"

Victoria replied, "I'm thinking about the Easter bunny."

"Oh really," said Fred, "and what are you thinking about the Easter bunny?" he probed.

She said, "Well, he's not real!"

Fred thought this might be a teachable moment—one of those moments when the distinction between fantasy and reality is made clear. So he pressed Victoria with another question. "And what about Santa Claus?" he inquired.

Victoria replied, "Oh, Santa doesn't think the Easter bunny is real, either."
—Stan Toler

GOOD ALL THE TIME

Asked why she said she liked Santa better than Jesus, a little girl replied, "You only have to be good at Christmas for Santa. But for Jesus, well, you have to be good for Him all the time." —Dennis J. Hester, comp., *The Vance Havner Quote Book* (Grand Rapids, MI: Baker Book House, 1986), p. 18.

FIVE FACTS OF CHRISTMAS

1. The exchanging of gifts is a custom that follows Christmas Day.
2. Peace on Earth means the toy is already broken.
3. The giver of a drum set is seldom appreciated.
4. People in your "Under five dollars" list probably didn't get you a gift.
5. The fine print in the warranty means nothing's covered unless it snows in Hawaii.
   —Jerry Brecheisen

WRONG CARD!

Getting a late start on the holidays, a lady hurriedly bought a box of identical Christmas cards from the sale table at the corner pharmacy.

With the post office mail deadline quickly approaching, she quickly signed, addressed, stamped and mailed the cards to 75 of her friends and relatives.

A few days later, her best friend called. "Sarah, I though we agreed not to exchange gifts this year."

"We did," Sarah replied. "I only sent you a card, just like we agreed."

"Did you read it?" her friend asked.

"I don't think so," she replied. "What did your card say?"

She read the message, "Just a note to say, a Christmas gift is on the way!" —Stan Toler

THREE WISE WOMEN?

Ever wonder what would have happened if it had been three wise women instead of three wise men? They would have asked directions, arrived on time, helped deliver the baby, cleaned up the stable, made a casserole and brought practical gifts.
—Author unknown

THE OTHER PERSON IN THE PLANE

A Sunday school teacher asked her students to draw a picture of the Bethlehem family. The drawing of one student surprised her: Mary, Joseph, and Baby Jesus were pictured riding in an airplane. The teacher inquired, "That's an interesting picture, Jimmy, but who's that other person in the plane?"

The little boy replied, "That's Pontius. He's the pilot." —Author unknown

WISE WORSHIP

My old friend Harry Childers once remarked, "After the wise men had truly worshiped, they opened their treasures." Hearing that, I made an important discovery on my journey to Christmas. You see, I had always wondered what happened to the gifts the wise men brought to the Son of God. Through Harry's observation I was reminded that God's guidance is perfect.

God sent Mary, Joseph and the Christ child to Bethlehem. When they arrived, they were in great need of food, finances and shelter. After Jesus' birth, they had moved from the lowly stable to a temporary home. It appeared that Satan's diabolical scheme for Herod to murder babies was going to succeed. But according to my friend Harry, after the wise men worshiped the Savior, they opened their treasures and unwittingly financed the flight of the Son of God to Egypt. Thus, they thwarted Herod's efforts to kill Mary's firstborn son.

Here's my discovery: Wise worship always leads to miracles, spiritual breakthroughs and provisions from the hand of almighty God! And wise worship only occurs when we, like the wise men, are willing to release our gifts to the Lord. Once that release has happened, we never know how the Father will use those gifts. —Stan Toler

ILLUSTRATIONS

THE GIFT OF FORGIVENESS

After describing a nostalgic Christmas Eve, with the family gathered together around the Christmas tree, singing carols, and eating Christmas goodies before attending the candlelight service, the author reminds us that for some families, Christmas Eve turns out to be a great battlefield with mines and torpedoes mixed. There is no peace on Earth, much less in the home. Expectations often run high and disappointments deep. The gift hoped for is the gift never given. The son who said he would be there—isn't. The sister who never has a kind word for anyone starts one of her many tirades.

Then he advises, "Wrap up one more gift and give it away—the gift of forgiveness. It may be the most important, and most beautiful, gift you will ever give to another person." —*Daylight Devotional Bible New International Version* (Grand Rapids, MI: Zondervan Publishing House, 1988), p. 1263.

THE ADVENT ADVENTURE

The words "Advent" and "adventure" have a common derivation. Advent should be a season of Christian adventure. As Christmas approaches, new hope and new faith enter our hearts. The adventure of life is renewed and reinvigorated. A spirit of expectancy and enthusiasm comes to those who remember the hope that God in Christ brings to man. —Charles L. Wallis, ed., *Speaker's Illustrations for Special Days* (New York: Abingdon Press, 1956), p. 62.

STEP OUT OF THE FRAME

A young boy, the son of missionaries, was living in a boarding school. Unable to visit his parents for the Christmas holidays, one of the dorm parents asked the boy what he wanted for Christmas.

He picked up a picture of his father from a stand by his bed, pointed to it, and said, "I want him to step out of that frame and stand by me." —E. Stanley Jones, quoted in *Speaker's Illustrations for Special Days,* ed. Charles L. Wallis (New York: Abingdon Press, 1956), p. 70.

FAMILY ADVENT WORSHIP

The Advent season is a time of celebration and hope. Gather your family and place an Advent wreath on the table. Within the evergreen circle place three purple candles, one rose-colored candle and a large white candle. The following worship schedule can then be observed:

Week One

Read Matthew 3:1,2; light a purple candle (representing prophecy) and have family prayer. Discuss expectations and hopes for the future.

Week Two

Read Matthew 2:1-6; light a purple candle (representing the shepherds) and have family prayer. Discuss anticipation and preparation for Christmas.

Week Three

Read Luke 2:8-12; light a rose-colored candle (representing the angels) and have family prayer. Discuss our joys in life.

Week Four

Read Matthew 2:7-11; light a purple candle (representing the Magi) and have family prayer. Discuss good gifts from the Father.

Christmas Day

Read John 8:12; light the white Christ candle and give thanks for Jesus, the Light of the World. —Linda Toler

CHRISTMAS IS COMING

In the comic strip *Garfield* by Jim Davis, Odie is asleep on the floor. Garfield walks up, lifts Odie's ear, and whispers, "Christmas is coming," then walks off. Odie is still asleep, but now there is a smile on his face and his tail is wagging ninety to nothing.

Christmas is coming and the excitement builds. The prophet speaks the words Jesus will read in his hometown and then proclaims, "Today this scripture has been fulfilled in your hearing" (Luke 4:21). —Michael Duduit, ed., *The Abingdon Preaching Annual 1997* (Nashville, TN: Abingdon Press, 1996), p. 80.

ADVENT'S TIMING CHAIN

One of the important parts of the automobile engine is the timing chain (or timing belts in newer cars). It connects the engine's crankshaft with the camshaft, ultimately making the pistons go up and down in the cylinders. In order for the engine to run smoothly, the camshaft opens and closes the valves, which must open and close at precise intervals. Their proper action means the engine is "in time."

Advent is the celebration of timing chain events that culminates in Christ's arrival just "in time." —Derl Keefer

ILLUSTRATIONS

STAR OR RATS?

Judy had one small but important part in the children's Christmas party. She was to hold up the word "STAR" at the appropriate time.

It seemed pretty simple—childproof, if you will. The letters were cut out and attached to a stick. Judy's assignment was to raise the stick with the letters S-T-A-R on it. When the time came, the little girl, right on cue, held the stick high. The audience roared with laughter.

At first the proud mother thought the congregation was appreciating her cute daughter. Then she realized why they were really laughing. You see, no one had told the little girl that there was a right way and a wrong way to hold the stick. Consequently, when she raised the stick, the sign was backward. Instead of saying S-T-A-R, the sign said R-A-T-S. —Stan Toler

POST OFFICE PREPARES FOR CHRISTMAS

Here's some good news out of Washington, DC: The post office says it is ready for the big holiday Christmas rush of mail. They have already placed an order for 10 million new signs that will read: This window closed. —David Letterman, *The Late Show with David Letterman* (December 1999).

HOLIDAY PLANS

One family was discussing their holiday plans. Father gave his plan: "Let's hang some things up."

"What things?" his teenage daughter asked.

He answered, "Mistletoe, stockings and the telephone!" —Author unknown

CHURCHES AND CHRISTMAS

Two friends were riding on a city bus. One of the riders saw a billboard sign sponsored by a local church: Keep Christ in Christmas.

"Well, have you ever?" the rider said to her friend. "Now the churches are sticking their noses into Christmas!" —Author unknown

CASH OR CREDIT?

My brother Terry often tells about a small child who had shopped all day with her Grandma. Grandma, seeking good behavior, promised a trip to see Santa at the end of the day. The little girl was good, and the reward was given. Santa gave the little a girl a candy cane.

"What do you say to Santa?" Grandma asked.

At first the little girl looked perplexed. Then with a knowing smile she said, "Charge it." —Stan Toler

MAIL ORDER GIFT

A father ordered a treehouse kit over the Internet just before Christmas. To his surprise, he opened the large packages to find a kit for building a sailboat.

Upset at the late date and the wrong delivery, he called the Internet company, "You sent the wrong catalog item! Now, what am I going to do?"

The representative replied very calmly, "Well, sir, I suggest you thank the Lord that you're not that fellow out on the lake trying to sail a treehouse." —Jeffrey Johnson

ILLUSTRATIONS

33

BAPTISM

Peter replied, "Repent and be baptized, every one of you, in the name of Jesus Christ for the forgiveness of your sins. And you will receive the gift of the Holy Spirit." Acts 2:38

There is no covert Christianity. Jesus commanded His followers to publicly witness their faith in Him. He, in turn, would bear that witness to His Father. In Peter's great Pentecost sermon, he reminded the seekers that they would openly follow the Savior.

In the days of John the Baptist, baptism was not merely a public declaration of faith in Christ. John preached a baptism of repentance—that is, people who were baptized by John were expressing sorrow for sin and symbolically being cleansed from their sins (see Mark 1:4). When Jesus came to be baptized, John was amazed. Not only was he unworthy to serve Jesus in this way, but John also knew that Jesus had never sinned and had no need to undergo the baptism of repentance.

It is at this point that Jesus symbolically introduces a new kind of baptism. Baptism for the New Testament Christian is a baptism signifying the finished work of Christ. This symbolic act demonstrates our death to our old selves, our identity with Jesus' burial and resurrection, and our present and future hope for redemption.

Over the last 2 millennia, millions of Christians have been baptized in the name of the Father, the Son and the Holy Spirit. The mode of baptism may differ, but the action is essentially the same. This sacred action demonstrates our blessed identity with Christ and is a public testimony to the life-changing work of the Holy Spirit.

SERMON SKETCH

THE BAPTISM OF A BELIEVER —STAN TOLER

MAIN TEXT: MATTHEW 28:16-20

Then the eleven disciples went to Galilee, to the mountain where Jesus had told them to go. When they saw him, they worshiped him; but some doubted. Then Jesus came to them and said, "All authority in heaven and on earth has been given to me. Therefore go and make disciples of all nations, baptizing them in the name of the Father and of the Son and of the Holy Spirit, and teaching them to obey everything I have commanded you. And surely I am with you always, to the very end of the age."

1. THE BIBLICAL BASIS FOR BAPTISM

Therefore go and make disciples of all nations, baptizing them in the name of the Father and of the Son and of the Holy Spirit (v. 19).

A. Baptism of Moses

For I do not want you to be ignorant of the fact, brothers, that our forefathers were all under the cloud and that they all passed through the sea. They were all baptized into Moses in the cloud and in the sea (1 Corinthians 10:1,2).

B. Baptism of John

I baptize you with water for repentance. But after me will come one who is more powerful than I, whose sandals I am not fit to carry. He will baptize you with the Holy Spirit and with fire (Matthew 3:11).

C. Baptism of Jesus

Jesus replied, "Let it be so now; it is proper for us to do this to fulfill all righteousness." Then John consented (Matthew 3:15).

SERMON
SKETCHES

2. THE TRUE MEANING OF A BELIEVER'S BAPTISM

A. Acceptance

"But what about you?" he asked. "Who do you say I am?" Simon Peter answered, "You are the Christ, the Son of the living God" (Matthew 16:15,16).

B. Confession

Therefore go and make disciples of all nations, baptizing them in the name of the Father and of the Son and of the Holy Spirit (Matthew 28:19).

C. Obedience

But if we walk in the light, as he is in the light, we have fellowship with one another, and the blood of Jesus, his Son, purifies us from all sin. If we claim to be without sin, we deceive ourselves and the truth is not in us. If we confess our sins, he is faithful and just and will forgive us our sins and purify us from all unrighteousness (1 John 1:7-9).

THE DECLARATION OF BAPTISM —JERRY BRECHEISEN

Praise be to the God and Father of our Lord Jesus Christ! In his great mercy he has given us new birth into a living hope through the resurrection of Jesus Christ from the dead (1 Peter 1:3).

1. I declare my faith: "Blessed be the Father of our Lord Jesus Christ."
2. I declare my forgiveness: "Who according to His great mercy has caused us to be born again."
3. I declare my future: "To a living hope through the resurrection of Jesus Christ from the dead."

QUOTES

A part of the act of baptism (for new members, not the ordination of ministers) in the Church of India is for the candidate to place his own hand on his head and say, "Woe is me if I preach not the gospel." —E. Paul Hovey, quoted in *12,000 Religious Quotations*, comp. Frank S. Mead (Grand Rapids, MI: Baker Book House, 1989), n.p.

By taking up the child into its life much as a mother embraces an infant, the baptismal act is the Church's affirmation of its maternal responsibility, a profession of its existence as a congregation. —Carl Michalson, "Why Methodists Baptize," *New Christian Advocate* (June 1958), n.p.

A BAPTISMAL STATEMENT

I take God to be my chief end and highest good.

I take God the Son to be my prince and Savior.

I take God the Holy Spirit to be my sanctifier, teacher, guide, and comforter.

I take the Word of God to be my rule in all my actions and the people of God to be my people under all conditions.

I do hereby dedicate and devote to the Lord all that I am, all that I have, and all I can do.

And this I do deliberately, freely and forever. —Father of Matthew Henry, quoted in Charles Swindoll, *The Tale of the Oxcart* (Nashville, TN: Word Publishing, 1998), p. 45.

Baptism signifies that the old Adam in us is to be drowned by daily sorrow and repentance, and perish with all sins and evil lusts; and that the new man should daily come forth again and rise, who shall live before God in righteousness and purity forever. —Martin Luther, "Luther's Small Catechism," quoted in *12,000 Religious Quotations*, comp. Frank S. Mead (Grand Rapids, MI: Baker Book House, 1989), n.p.

Baptism is the declaration of the universal face of the sonship of man to God. —Phillips Brooks, quoted in *Inspiring Quotations*, comp. Albert Wells, Jr. (Nashville, TN: Thomas Nelson Publishing, 1988). n.p.

QUOTES

Being by nature born in sin, and the children of wrath, we are hereby made the children of grace. —"Book of Common Prayer: The Catechism," in *12,000 Religious Quotations*, comp. Frank S. Mead (Grand Rapids, MI: Baker Book House, 1989), n.p.

The person being baptized experiences the firm support of the community—of the Body of Christ—in the arms and hands of the minister, feels the plunge of commitment, and bursts into new life with the sound and feel of rushing water. —Author unknown. http://www.disciples.org/baplief.html (accessed September 1999).

We may never be martyrs but we can die to self, to sin, to the world, to our plans and ambitions. That is the significance of baptism; we died with Christ and rose to a new life. —Vance Havner, quoted in *The Vance Havner Quote Book*, comp. Dennis J. Hester (Grand Rapids, MI: Baker Book House, 1986), p. 13.

The efficacy of baptism is not tied to that moment of time wherein it is administered. —The Westminster Confession of Faith

ILLUSTRATIONS

BAPTISM IS LIKE A WEDDING RING

Baptism is like a wedding ring: they both symbolize transactions. A wedding ring symbolizes marriage, just as baptism symbolizes salvation. Wearing a wedding ring does not make you married any more than being baptized makes you saved. —*The Autoillustrator*. http://www.biblestudytools.net/SermonHelps/AutoIllustrator/index.cgi (no access date).

TOO MUCH BAPTISM

Concerned that the preacher was preaching on the subject of baptism too regularly, the deacons suggested he change subjects.

"Give me another subject, then, and I'll give it a try," the preacher responded.

They suggested Genesis 1.

The next Sunday, the preacher began his message, "I've been requested to preach from Genesis 1. I like that because it suggests that when the Lord created our planet, He made most of it water, and that sorta reminds me of baptism." —Roy B. Zuck, comp., *The Speaker's Quote Book* (Grand Rapids, MI: Kregel Publishing, 1997), p. 70.

THE NARROW ROAD

A missionary was trying to explain what it means to follow Christ. "The Christian life is like walking a narrow road."

His student replied with wisdom beyond his years, "Yes, a narrow road. There is only room for one: Christ in me." —Author unknown

THE BAPTISM OF CHARLES HADDON SPURGEON

Charles Haddon Spurgeon was reared in a Congregational home. Both his father and grandfather were preachers. He was baptized on his mother's birthday, the water and weather were so cold that a fire was built by the people standing on the banks so they could keep warm. Spurgeon, then sixteen, had walked eight miles that morning to be baptized.

Later, he not only preached to great throngs in London's 5,000-seat Metropolitan Tabernacle, but for forty years in England, Europe, and America, his sermons sold 150 million copies. In addition, he wrote 135 books that were translated into many languages. —J. B. Fowler, Jr., *Illustrating Great Words of the New Testament*, (Nashville, TN: Broadman Press, 1991), n.p.

Illustrations

Painful Silence

It is said that when St. Patrick baptized King Aengus in the fifth century, he accidentally stabbed the king's foot with his pointed staff. Following the baptism, St. Patrick noticed blood on the water and realized what he did.

"Sire, why did you suffer such pain in silence?" he asked.

The king answered, "I thought it was part of the baptism." —"Baptism," *Sermon Illustrations.com*, 1999. http://www.sermonillustrations.com/a-z/b/baptism.html (accessed December 2000).

I Would Give My Life

The great pianist Paderweski finished his performance and was greeted by one of his fans. "I would give my life to play the piano like that!"

Paderwski responded, "I have done just that, sir." —Author unknown

Baptism Practice

After the baptism of their young boy, the pastor commented to the parents who were farmers, "I was expecting a few problems. But that boy of yours certainly went through baptism with flying colors!"

The parents replied, "Well, pastor, that's because we've been practicing on him. Once a week, my husband has been dunking him in the watering tank in the barnyard." —Lowell D. Streiker, comp., *An Encyclopedia of Humor* (Peabody, MA: Hendrickson Publishers, 1998), p. 82.

Seeker-Sensitive Baptism

Two elderly members were discussing the newest trends in worship. "I just can't believe it. Our church is talking about adding a drive-in service," one disgruntled lady commented.

Her friend replied, "Oh, I know it! But when they start doing baptisms at the car wash, I'm outta here!" —Bob Phillips, ed., *The World's All-Time Best Collection of Good Clean Jokes* (New York: Galahad Books, 1996), p. 51.

More Water, Please

The pastor guided the young candidate into the baptismal pool. "Your full name?" The pastor asked.

"Edward Jeffrey Charles Martin Mackenzie the Third," the boy loudly announced.

The custodian shouted, "Hold it, Preacher! I'll go get some more water!" —Bob Phillips, ed., *The World's All-Time Best Collection of Good Clean Jokes* (New York: Galahad Books, 1996), p. 49.

IMMERSED OR SPRINKLED?

A Presbyterian and a Baptist minister were having an intense discussion about baptism. The Baptist minister insisted that the candidates should be fully immersed, while the Presbyterian minister opted for sprinkling. The Presbyterian minister asked some qualifying questions.

"Is he baptized if he is in water up to his chin?"

"No," the Baptist minister replied.

"Up to his nose?" asked the Presbyterian.

Again the response, "No."

"How about up to his eyebrows?"

"No," the Baptist minister insisted.

"His eyebrows?"

"No," the Baptist minister responded. "He must have his whole head under water!"

"See," the Presbyterian minister added, "it's the water on top of his head that counts!" —Eleanor Doan, comp., *The Speaker's Sourcebook* (Grand Rapids, MI: Zondervan Publishing House, 1960), p. 30.

FATHER MURPHY WASHED MY SINS AWAY

"It's time for your bath," a mother announced to her boy. "Cleanliness is next to godliness."

"In that case, I'll never have to take a bath!"

"How's that?" the mother inquired.

The boy answered, "Cause you told me that when I was a baby, Father Murphy held me in his arms and washed my sins away." —Angelo J. Mongiore and Melvin E. Schroer, *A Funny Thing Happened* (New York: The Pilgrim Press, 1991), p. 29.

CAT BAPTISM

The four-year-old daughter of a preacher was conducting a "baptism" in the backyard. She picked up a cat and held it over a rain barrel.

Trying to mimic her father, she placed the cat in the barrel and said, "I baptize you in the name of the Father, the Son, and in the hole-you-go." —Charles Foster, quoted in "A Child's View," *Focus on the Family Magazine.* http://www.sermons.org/illustrations.html (no access date).

CALL ME BUBBA

A minister was baptizing a five-year-old boy. When he announced his name, "Roger Edward Junior," the little boy interrupted. "Mister, I'm a third not a junior, and if it's all right with you, I'd rather you call me 'Bubba.'" —Eleanor Doan, comp., *The Speaker's Sourcebook* (Grand Rapids, MI: Zondervan Publishing House, 1960), n.p.

41

BAPTIZED AT GRAMMA'S

"I was baptized at Gramma's," the six-year-old announced after returning from a stay at his grandparents' house.

"You were baptized at Gramma's?" his mother responded. "Tell me about it."

The little boy spoke excitedly, "It was wonderful, Mom! When I took my bath, I put my head under the water and thought about Jesus!" —Author unknown

WE'LL LOAN YOU THE TUB

The minister of a different denomination contacted the pastor of a large Baptist church and made an unusual request. He had several folks who had recently joined his church who preferred to be baptized by immersion rather than sprinkling, the church's normal mode of baptism. The minister requested the use of their baptistry *and* the Baptist pastor himself. This posed a dilemma—what if those being baptized weren't born again? Wishing to handle his answer with tact, he wrote the pastor, "We don't take in laundry, but we'll be happy to loan you our tub." —Charles R. Swindoll, *The Grace Awakening* (Nashville, TN: Word Publishing, 1996), p. 72.

THE LUTHERAN PASTOR'S FIRST BAPTISM

The new pastor at the Lutheran church asked the pastor at First Baptist Church if he could use the baptismal tank. Three people from the Lutheran church had requested baptism by immersion.

The Lutheran pastor was unfamiliar with the ceremony so he asked the host pastor for some tips. "I make a few comments," the pastor offered, "and then I carefully bend the person back under the water."

The preliminaries went well, but there was a problem when he baptisms began. The Lutheran minister put the candidates under the water first—and made his lengthy comments while they were there. A loud gasp was heard when each candidate surfaced. —Barry Kolamowski, quoted in *Dynamic Illustrations*, comp. King Duncan (Knoxville, TN: Seven Worlds Publishing, 1996), p. 16.

COMMUNION

~

TO HONOR AND PROCLAIM

And he took bread, gave thanks and broke it, and gave it to them, saying,
"This is my body given for you; do this in remembrance of me." Luke 22:19

The Lord's Supper is a symbolic observance to honor Christ's death and resurrection. The first Communion was observed the night before the Jewish Passover. The Passover commemorated the Jews' deliverance from slavery and God's gracious provision for their escape. Similarly, the Lord's Supper commemorates our own deliverance from slavery in sin and God's gracious provision for our escape from eternal damnation.

The Communion elements include unleavened bread and wine. The unleavened bread represents the sinless body of Christ. The wine represents the shed blood of Christ. After Christ had broken the bread, He exhorted His disciples to eat it "in [His] remembrance." Following the bread, Jesus took the wine and exhorted His disciples to also drink it in remembrance of Him.

In 1 Corinthians 11, the apostle Paul teaches that we must accept the Lord's Supper in a manner worthy of the Lord. We are to come to the Communion table knowledgeably and purposefully, and we should examine our hearts for sin. Communion is an opportunity for worship as we focus on God's sacrificial gift to us. By participating in these symbolic activities, we are joining others in proclaiming the Lord's death until He comes (see 1 Corinthians 11:26).

43

SERMON
SKETCHES

SERMON SKETCHES

FIVE PRINCIPLES OF COMMUNION —L. GUY NEES, THE PREACHING MAGAZINE (OCTOBER 2, 1983), N.P.

MAIN TEXT: 1 CORINTHIANS 10:16,17; 11:24-28

1. Unification (see 1 Corinthians 10:16,17)

2. Separation (see 1 Corinthians 10:18-21)

3. Commemoration (see 1 Corinthians 11:24-26)

4. Examination (see 1 Corinthians 11:27,28)

5. Prediction (see 1 Corinthians 11:16)

A SIGNIFICANT SACRAMENT —ELMER TOWNS

MAIN TEXT: 1 CORINTHIANS 11:24-29

1. A Wonderful Remembrance (see vv. 24, 25)

2. A New Testament Requirement (see v. 26)

3. A Testimony of Faith (see v. 26)

4. A Feast of Dedication (see v. 28, 29)

WHAT IS THE LORD'S SUPPER? —STAN TOLER

MAIN TEXT: 1 CORINTHIANS 11:23-26
1. The Lord's Supper is a memorial service (v. 24: "do this in remembrance").
    a. We're to remember *that* He died.
    b. We're to remember *why* He died.
    c. We're to remember *how* He died.
2. The Lord's Supper is a time of communion (see 1 Corinthians 10:16,17).
    a. Communion with the Lord
    b. Communion with the Lord's people
3. The Lord's Supper is a time for examination (see 1 Corinthians 11:28,29).

4. The Lord's Supper is a time to give thanks (see v. 24).

5. The Lord's Supper is a time for proclamation (see v. 26).

THE LORD'S SUPPER —STAN TOLER

MAIN TEXT: 1 CORINTHIANS 11:23-33

1. Look back at what He did (see vv. 23-25).

2. Look ahead until He comes (see v. 26).

3. Look within your own heart (see vv. 27-29).

4. Look around to help others (see v. 33).

THE COMMUNION LOOK —JERRY BRECHEISEN

MAIN TEXT: 1 CORINTHIANS 11:23-26

1. The Upward Look (see v. 24)

2. The Inward Look (see v. 25)

3. The Outward Look (see v. 26)

HOW TO PROPERLY OBSERVE THE LORD'S SUPPER —STAN TOLER

1. Come to the table with sincere appreciation:
   Jesus took bread, gave thanks and broke it (see Matthew 26:26).

2. Come to the table with self-examination:
   A man ought to examine himself (see 1 Corinthians 11:28).

3. Come to the table with brotherly consideration:
   One loaf, one body (see 1 Corinthians 10:17).

SERMON SKETCHES

45

QUOTES

QUOTES

At Passover, only the blood of the lamb on the doorposts would save the children of Israel. The character or the good works of the people inside the household didn't matter. This is a foreshadowing of salvation through faith alone. —Harold Lindsell, ed., *Harper Study Bible* (Grand Rapids, MI: Zondervan Publishing House, 1972), p. 98.

The Lord's Supper is not simply a memorial of the Last Supper, nor of Christ's death per se. It is a constant, repeated reminder—and experience—of the efficacy of that death for *us*, not just for *me*. Salvation through Christ's death has created a new community of people who bear His name. —Gordon D. Fee, "How Not to Celebrate Communion," *The Preacher's Magazine* (June/July/August 1996), p. 22.

Holy Communion is the feast of the Kingdom. Unless we consciously seek God's rule in all things concerning our lives, this feast is empty and void. —Lloyd Ogilvie

Communion is never irrelevant, because it is always rooted and grounded in real history. It is the memory of real events. —Robert Holland, "Barnyard Echoes," *Preaching Today*, no. 14 (1987), audiocassette.

The Communion table combines the remembering power of all the senses—sight and sound and touch and taste and aroma—those are Aristotle's five. But let me add to the aroma one other: atmosphere. This table is within an atmosphere that makes it sacred. It is here, in this sacred place, that some of you have said to me at times, "Don't let the children run in the church." It must be that you feel a special, holy atmosphere here. And Communion wouldn't be the same down in the furnace room, because the atmosphere would be wrong. —Robert Holland, "Barnyard Echoes," *Preaching Today*, no. 14 (1987), audiocassette.

True worship comes by Calvary. If Calvary and Christ's dying love mean nothing to you, no matter what your religion may be, you cannot worship God. —William Ford, *Glimpses of Glory* (New York: Loizeaux Bros., 1949), p. 31.

The Lord's Supper literally celebrates life, provides spiritual nourishment, and proclaims hope. The Communion meal is designed for people who cry—bruised and hurt—but also for those who rejoice, laugh, and giggle. —Jerry Hull, "Let Us Celebrate Communion," *The Preacher's Magazine* (October 1977), p. 15.

46

ILLUSTRATIONS

COMMUNION KINDNESS

A Sunday school teacher knelt beside the nine-year-old at the communion rail. She sensed the boy's nervousness as he handled the chrome tray of tiny glasses. As he took one of the glasses, he accidentally brushed the tray, spilling its contents on the altar.

With kindness and grace, the Sunday school teacher quickly took out her embroidered handkerchief and wiped the pool of grape juice. She then poured the contents of her cup into the boy's cup, and continued as if nothing had happened. —George Lyons, "How Not to Celebrate Communion," *The Preacher's Magazine* (June/July/August 1996), p. 22.

COMMUNION SERVICE LIKE A BOY SCOUT CAMPFIRE MEAL

The elements of a Boy Scout campfire meal might be instructive for leading an effective Communion service. A wise pastor will attempt to approximate this model.

Boy Scouts: 1) Excitedly anticipate the meal; 2) Almost push and crowd in order to satiate their hunger; 3) Gratefully thank those who make the arrangements; 4) Eat in a spirit of relaxed camaraderie and 5) Cherish vivid memories about both the adequacy of nourishment and pleasure of the meal. —Jerry Hull, "Let Us Celebrate Communion," *The Preacher's Magazine* (October 1977), p. 15.

FIRST COMMUNION

A three-year-old took her first communion. The pastor patted her on the head as he gave her the elements, "God be with you."

When she got home she pretended to serve communion to her dolls. Her mother watched as she passed pieces of bread to each of the dolls, patted them on the head and said softly, "God will get you." —Derl Keefer

ILLUSTRATIONS

IMAGINARY COMMUNION

In the book *Visions of a World Hungry*, Thomas G. Pettepiece tells of being held as a political prisoner. On Easter Sunday, many of his fellow prisoners wanted to participate in a communion service.

Placing imaginary bread in the empty hands of the prisoners, he said "Take, eat, this is my body which is given for you; do this in remembrance of me." With bowed heads, the prisoners pretended to put the "bread" into their mouths.

From his empty palm, he then took the "cup" and placed it into their hands, one by one. "Take, drink, this is the blood of Christ which was shed for you. Let us give thanks, knowing that Christ is in this very room.

After they "drank" the "cup" they sang a song of praise, embraced, and went back to their prison cell. —Thomas G. Pettepiece, *Vision of a World Hungry* (Nashville, TN: Upper Room, 1979), p. 14.

THE GALLOWS MEAL

I discovered something about the Last Supper recently that I had not fully comprehended before. I was watching Stanley Kubrick's classic film, "Paths of Glory," on late television. I was deeply struck by the scene of the "gallows meal," the final meal the prisoners shared before their execution. And I realized that the Last Supper was that type of meal: a very emotional occasion, when all superficiality is put aside, when only the most meaningful and honest things are said and done. —William Toohey, *Fully Alive* (St. Meinrad, IN: Abbey Press, 1976), p. 28.

THEY DIDN'T GIVE HIM MUCH

One weekend my little brother was visiting our grandparents in another town. They took him to church with them, and on Sunday after church, he asked what Communion was all about.

Granddad replied, "That was Jesus' last supper."

My little brother replied, "Boy, they didn't give him much, did they?" —Elaine Boreber and Edward K. Rowell, *Humor for Preaching and Teaching* (Grand Rapids, MI: Baker Book House, 1996), p. 64.

48

EASTER

With great power the apostles continued to testify to the resurrection of the Lord Jesus, and much grace was upon them all. Acts 4:33

A HISTORY OF THE EASTER CELEBRATION

For the Christian, Easter is a glorious holy day. On this day, we commemorate the redemptive death and resurrection of Jesus Christ, the Son of God. We stand firmly on the fact that Jesus came back to life after suffering a horrific death of crucifixion. On the first day of the week, early in the morning, Mary Magdalene came to the tomb in which Christ was buried to anoint Him with spices (see Luke 24:1). She discovered the empty tomb; and word quickly spread that Jesus had, indeed, victoriously overcome death.

Easter allows the church to continue to spread the word of Jesus' resurrection. Its celebration activities not only reaffirm the faith of those who participate, it also witnesses to the saving power of the Lord Jesus Christ.

The name "Easter" derives its name from old Teutonic mythology. The Anglo-Saxon goddess of spring and offspring had the names of Ostara or Eostre.[1] This annual festival to spring coincided with the Christian celebration of Easter, so when early Christian missionaries came through the Teutonic tribes, they merely transformed the festival into one of Christian significance.[2] In A.D. 325 Emperor Constantine scheduled the official celebration of Easter on the first Sunday after the first full moon after the vernal equinox. Easter is therefore bound never to fall before March 22 or after April 25.[3]

49

SERMON SKETCHES

THE OTHER DISCIPLE —ELMER TOWNS

MAIN TEXT: JOHN 20:1-18

*Both were running, but the other disciple outran Peter and reached the tomb first.
John 20:4*

1. He ran out of curiosity.

*So she came running to Simon Peter and the other disciple, the one Jesus loved, and said,
"They have taken the Lord out of the tomb, and we don't know where they have put
him!" (v. 2).*

2. He ran out of courtesy.

He bent over and looked in at the strips of linen lying there but did not go in (v. 5).

3. He ran out of loyalty.

*Finally the other disciple, who had reached the tomb first, also went inside. He saw and
believed. (They still did not understand from Scripture that Jesus had to rise from the
dead) (vv. 8,9).*

4. He ran in victory.

Then the disciples went back to their homes (v. 10).

WHAT A DIFFERENCE A DAY MAKES —JERRY BRECHEISEN

MAIN TEXT: MATTHEW 28:1-10

1. What looked like a last day turned to a first day.

*After the Sabbath, at dawn on the first day of the week, Mary Magdalene and the other
Mary went to look at the tomb (v. 1).*

2. What looked like a day of defeat turned to a day of victory.

There was a violent earthquake, for an angel of the Lord came down from heaven and, going to the tomb, rolled back the stone and sat on it (v. 2).

3. What looked like a memorial day turned to the Lord's Day.

He is not here; he has risen, just as he said. Come and see the place where he lay. Then go quickly and tell his disciples: "He has risen from the dead and is going ahead of you into Galilee. There you will see him." Now I have told you (vv. 6,7).

THE WONDERFUL JOURNEYS OF JESUS —JERRY BRECHEISEN

MAIN TEXT: JOHN 1:29

The next day John saw Jesus coming toward him and said, "Look, the Lamb of God, who takes away the sin of the world!"

1. The Journey of the Cradle

The Word became flesh and made his dwelling among us. We have seen his glory, the glory of the One and Only who came from the Father, full of grace and truth (John 1:14).

2. The Journey of the Crown

The next day the great crowd that had come for the Feast heard that Jesus was on his way to Jerusalem. They took palm branches and went out to meet him, shouting, "Hosanna! Blessed is he who comes in the name of the Lord! Blessed is the King of Israel!" (John 12:12,13).

3. The Journey of the Cross

Finally Pilate handed him over to them to be crucified. So the soldiers took charge of Jesus. Carrying his own cross, he went out to the place of the Skull (which in Aramaic is called Golgotha). Here they crucified him, and with him two others—one on each side and Jesus in the middle (John 19:16-18).

SERMON
SKETCHES

PALM SUNDAY: PALMS OF VICTORY —STAN TOLER

MAIN TEXT: MATTHEW 21:8,9

A very large crowd spread their cloaks on the road, while others cut branches from the trees and spread them on the road. The crowds that went ahead of him and those that followed shouted, "Hosanna to the Son of David! Blessed is he who comes in the name of the Lord! Hosanna in the highest!"

1. The Preparation for the King

    If anyone asks you, "Why are you doing this?" tell him, "The Lord needs it and will send it back here shortly." They went and found a colt outside in the street, tied at a doorway. As they untied it, some people standing there asked, "What are you doing, untying that colt?" They answered as Jesus had told them to, and the people let them go (Mark 11:3-6).

2. The Prophesy of His Entry

    Rejoice greatly, O Daughter of Zion! Shout, Daughter of Jerusalem! See, your king comes to you, righteous and having salvation, gentle and riding on a donkey, on a colt, the foal of a donkey (Zechariah 9:9).

3. The Powerful Procession

    A very large crowd spread their cloaks on the road, while others cut branches from the trees and spread them on the road (Matthew 21:8).

4. The Exciting Entry

    The crowds that went ahead of him and those that followed shouted, "Hosanna to the Son of David! Blessed is he who comes in the name of the Lord! Hosanna in the highest!" (Matthew 21:9).

    A. Gladness
    B. Praise

QUOTES

NEW HERE AND NOW

The great Easter truth is not that we are to live newly after death—that is not the great thing—but that we are to be new here and now by the power of the Resurrection. —Phillips Brooks, quoted in *Illustrations Unlimited*, comp. James Hewett (Wheaton, IL: Tyndale House, 1988), n.p.

At one time people thought the world was flat. Columbus sailed his boats and a stone was rolled away. The world was changed forever. —King Duncan, comp., "Reality Maps and Rolling Stones," *Dynamic Preaching*, vol. X, no. 4 (April 1995), n.p.

> Love's redeeming work is done.
> Fought the fight, the battle won.
> Death in vain forbids him rise
> Christ has opened paradise. —Charles Wesley, quoted in *Inspiring Quotations*, ed. Albert Wells, Jr. (Nashville, TN: Thomas Nelson, 1988), n.p.

I don't know anybody who can contemplate his own death and hum a tune at the same time. —Woody Allen, quoted in *Dynamic Preaching*, vol. X, no. 4, comp. King Duncan (April 1995), n.p.

Easter is the New Year's Day of the soul. —A. B. Simpson, quoted in *Inspiring Quotations*, ed. Albert Wells, Jr. (Nashville, TN: Thomas Nelson, 1988), n.p.

Easter is the morning when the Lord laughs out loud, laughs at all the things that snuff out joy, all the things that pretend to be all-powerful, like cruelty and madness and despair and evil, and most especially, that great pretender, death. —Frank Yates, quoted in *Holy Humor, Inspirational Wit and Cartoons*, ed. Cal and Rose Samra (Nashville, TN: Thomas Nelson, 1997), n.p.

The resurrection never becomes a fact of experience until the risen Lord lives in the heart of the believer. —Peter Marshall, quoted in *Inspiring Quotations*, ed. Albert Wells, Jr. (Nashville, TN: Thomas Nelson, 1988), n.p.

QUOTES

The heavy, ponderous stone that sealed Jesus in the confines of that rock-walled tomb was but a pebble compared to the Rock of Ages inside.
—James Hewett, "Easter," *Illustrations Unlimited,* comp. James Hewett (Wheaton, IL: Tyndale House, 1988), p. 164.

Our Lord has written the promise of resurrection, not in books alone, but in every leaf of springtime. —Martin Luther

OUR ENEMIES ARE BEATEN

The Easter message tells us that our enemies, sin, the curse, and death, are beaten. Ultimately they can no longer start mischief. They still behave as though the game were not decided, the battle not fought; we must still reckon with them, but fundamentally we must cease to fear them any more.
—Karl Barth, "Dogmatics in Outline," *Illustrations Unlimited,* comp. James Hewett (Wheaton, IL: Tyndale House, 1988), p. 168.

Observing Easter without Good Friday teaches a half-truth. —Keith Drury

ILLUSTRATIONS

A SIGN FOR JESUS

The deaf have a sign for Jesus. The middle finger of each hand is placed into the palm of the other. Jesus, the one with the wounded hands. And when they touch the place, they remember. They hear the name in their own flesh. —John Vannorsdall, quoted in *Illustrations Unlimited*, comp. James Hewett (Wheaton, IL: Tyndale House, 1988), p. 165.

THE CROWN OF LIFE

Crowns have always been the sign of authority and royalty. Richard the Lion Heart had a crown so heavy that two earls had to stand, one on either side, to hold his head. Edward II once owned nine crowns. The crown that Queen Elizabeth wears is worth over $20 million.

All of them are but trinkets compared to Christ's crown. It was not formed by skilled craftsmen. It was put together hurriedly by the rough hands of Roman soldiers. I deserved to wear it. He took my crown of thorns, and offered to me instead His crown of life. —James Hewett, comp., *Illustrations Unlimited* (Wheaton, IL: Tyndale House, 1988), p. 163.

THE COFFIN REMINDER

It is said that the great actress Sarah Bernhardt always kept a coffin at the foot of her bed so she could see it when she awoke. She explained, "This is to remind me that my body will soon be dust and that my glory alone will live forever." —King Duncan, ed., "Reality Maps and Rolling Stones," *Dynamic Preaching*, vol. X, no. 4 (April 1995), p. 27.

HE TOOK THE STING

A little boy and his father were playing catch. Suddenly a honeybee swarmed over the boy. The father reacted quickly. His son was highly allergic to bee stings. One sting could prove fatal.

The boy cried out as the father grabbed for the honeybee and caught it in his hand.

Then he let it go.

"Dad!" the boy protested, "why did you let it go?"

His father replied, "It's harmless now."

"How do you know?" the son asked.

"Look here, son," the father pointed to his hand, "I took the sting. The stinger is still in my hand. —James Hewett, comp., *Illustrations Unlimited* (Wheaton, IL: Tyndale House, 1988), n.p.

ILLUSTRATIONS

DISTINGUISHING THE SPIRITUAL FROM THE RITUAL

A very small and very devout boy was heard murmuring to himself on Easter morning a poem of his own composition, which began, "Chocolate eggs and Jesus risen." This seems to me, for his age, both admirable poetry and admirable piety.

But, of course, the time will soon come when such a child can no longer effortlessly and spontaneously enjoy that unity. He will become able to distinguish the spiritual from the ritual and festal aspect of Easter; chocolate eggs will no longer be sacramental. And, once he has distinguished, he must put one or the other first. If he puts the spiritual first, he can still taste something of Easter in the chocolate eggs; if he puts the eggs first, they will soon be no more than any other sweetmeat. They have taken on an independent and, therefore, a soon-withering life. —C.S. Lewis, "Reflections on the Psalms," *Pastor's Weekly Briefing*, vol. 6, no. 15 (April 10, 1998), p. 2.

WHAT DID SHE GET FOR EASTER?

Grandfather asked his granddaughter what her neighbor friend got for Easter.

"Grandpa," she replied, "she didn't get anything! She's Jewish."

She added, "It's like this, Grandpa: I'm Christmas, and she's Hanukkah. I'm Easter, and she's Passover."

Grandpa replied, "Thank you, honey, that clears it up for me."

"Oh, I forgot one other thing, Grandpa," the granddaughter said.

"What's that?"

She answered with a smile, "Praise the Lord, we're both Halloween!" —Buddy Westbrook, quoted in Loyal Jones, *The Preacher's Joke Book* (Little Rock, AR: August House, 1989), p. 26

THAT SAME HYMN

A parishioner shook hands with her pastor after the service and commended him on his sermon.

"I have one small complaint," she added.

"And what's that?" the pastor replied.

"Well, every time I come to this church, they always sing the same hymn!"

"Which one is that?" the pastor inquired.

She replied agitated, "Christ the Lord Is Risen Today!" —King Duncan, comp., *Dynamic Preaching*, vol. X, no. 4 (April 1995), p. 25.

EASTER PLANTS

During the Sunday morning children's sermon, the pastor asked the young parishioners if they knew what plant was used to symbolize Easter.

A little boy raised his hand, "Pastor, I'm not real sure, but I think it's an eggplant." —Angela Akers and King Duncan, eds., *Amusing Grace* (Knoxville, TN: Seven Worlds Corporation, 1993), p. 304.

BEYOND THE CROSS

The Stations of the Cross is a tourist attraction in the Italian Alps. Visitors climb a mountain to stand beside an outdoor crucifix. One tourist noticed a trail that led beyond that cross. Fighting rough thicket, she made her way down the small trail. She was surprised to find another shrine. Brush had nearly covered it. It was neglected because visitors had only gone as far as the cross.

Too many have stopped at the cross. They haven't moved beyond its despair and heartbreak to find the real message of Easter: the empty tomb. —Lavon Brown, "Easter," *Illustrations Unlimited*, comp. James Hewett (Wheaton, IL: Tyndale House, 1988), p. 164.

THE PRESENCE OF A RISEN CHRIST

A Lutheran bishop in Hungary was imprisoned six years for protesting the confiscating of church schools by the Communist regime.

"They placed me in solitary confinement," he told a Minneapolis assembly. "It was a tiny cell, perhaps six feet by eight feet, with no windows, and soundproofed."

He added, "They hoped to break down my resistance by isolating me from all sensory perceptions. They thought I was alone. They were wrong. The risen Christ was present in that room, and in communion with Him, I was able to prevail." —Andrew Wyermann, "Easter," *Illustrations Unlimited*, comp. James Hewett (Wheaton, IL: Tyndale House, 1988), p. 165.

THE MEANING OF EASTER

Three-year-old Nicole was anxious for Easter to come. "I can't wait for Easter, Daddy!"

"Do you know what Easter means, honey?"

With arms raised, a smile on her face, and at the top of her voice she said, "Surprise!"

What better word could sum up the meaning of Easter? Surprise, death! Surprise, sin! Surprise, mourning disciples! Surprise, modern man! He's alive! —James Hewett, comp., *Illustrations Unlimited* (Wheaton, IL: Tyndale House, 1988), p. 162.

FUNERALS

FUNERAL SERVICE

Since the children have flesh and blood, he too shared in their humanity so that by his death he might destroy him who holds the power of death—that is, the devil—and free those who all their lives were held in slavery by their fear of death. Hebrews 2:14,15

From the most primitive history until today, humans of all races and cultures have formally performed rites of passage from life to death. Christ's own death and burial is described in the four Gospels, and today we still commemorate His suffering and departure from this earth. But the Christian who participates in a funeral can have a perspective on death that is different from anyone else's.

The purpose of the funeral is to commend the dead to the mercies of God.[1] This means that even for the funeral of a nonbeliever, Christians can affirm hope and trust in God to judge their loved one righteously. The Christian has the unique opportunity to view the funeral as a means of proclaiming the gospel. We know of Christ's death and sufferings, but we also know of His resurrection. Where there is no death, there can be no resurrection.[2]

The hope found in the resurrection of Christ does not belittle the mourning that even the most devout believer may suffer. Even Jesus mourned the death of His friend Lazarus (see John 11:35). The funeral is appropriately a time of both grieving and rejoicing—a celebration of death and of life. Jesus' victory over death is our comfort.

58

SERMON SKETCHES

LESSON FROM SPARROWS —JERRY BRECHEISEN

TEXT: MATTHEW 10:29-31

Are not two sparrows sold for a penny? Yet not one of them will fall to the ground apart from the will of your Father. And even the very hairs of your head are all numbered. So don't be afraid; you are worth more than many sparrows.

1.   God sees (v. 29).
2.   God knows (v. 30).
3.   God cares (v. 31).

THE GOOD SHEPHERD —ELMER TOWNS

TEXT: PSALM 23

A psalm of David.
      The LORD is my shepherd, I shall not be in want. He makes me lie down in green pastures, he leads me beside quiet waters, he restores my soul. He guides me in the paths of righteousness for his name's sake. Even though I walk through the valley of the shadow of death, I will fear no evil, for you are with me; your rod and your staff, they comfort me. You prepare a table before me in the presence of my enemies. You anoint my head with oil; my cup overflows. Surely goodness and love will follow me all the days of my life, and I will dwell in the house of the LORD forever.

1.   The Good Shepherd cares about us individually and we know Him.
2.   The Good Shepherd cares about us in difficult times.
3.   The Good Shepherd cares about us enough to bring to us His peace.
4.   The Good Shepherd cares about us enough to bring us to heaven.

THE DEATH OF ABRAHAM —JERRY BRECHEISEN

TEXT: GENESIS 25:7,8

Altogether, Abraham lived a hundred and seventy-five years. Then Abraham breathed his last and died at a good old age, an old man and full of years; and he was gathered to his people.

1.   Abraham breathed his last and died.
2.   Abraham was an old man, satisfied with life.
3.   Abraham was gathered to his people.

QUOTES

QUOTES

CROSSING THE BAR

Sunset and evening star,
And one clear call for me!
And may there be no moaning at the bar,
When I put out to sea.

But such a tide as moving seems asleep,
Too full for sound and foam,
When that which drew from out the boundless deep,
Turns again home.

Twilight and evening bell,
And after that the dark!
And may there be no sadness of farewell,
When I embark.

For though from out our bourne of Time and Place
The flood may bear me far,
I hope to see my Pilot face to face
When I have crossed the bar. —Alfred Lord Tennyson

THE INTERLUDE

Death
Is a soft interlude
Between the noises of time
And the solitude of eternity;

Its melody is penned
By the Heavenly Composer,
And performed by earthly
Musicians,
Who play its score
With chords of faith
Or discords of unbelief;
In a somber rehearsal
Of an everlasting
Symphony. —Jerry Brecheisen

IN A MOMENT

In a moment,
In one glorious moment,
Every sigh,
Every wincing expression of humanity's hurt
Will be wrapped in a package of sun-filled clouds
And tossed on the shores of evermore.

Then God
Will pick it up,
As would a potter,
Unwrap the clouds,
And remold its contents
Into a vessel
Fit for the mantles
Of heaven. —Jerry Brecheisen

DIARY OF AN OLD SOUL

I rise and run, staggering-double and run.
But whither-whither-whither for escape?
The sea lies all about this long-necked cape—
There come the dogs, straight for me every one—
Me, live despair, live center of alarms!
Ah, lo, 'twixt me and all his barking harms,
The Shepherd, lo, I run-fall folded in his arms. —George
MacDonald, *Diary of an Old Soul*, quoted by Dave Hansen,
"Cloud of Witnesses," *Leadership Journal* (Winter 1997).
http://www.christianity.net/leadership7L1/7L1105.html
(accessed October 4, 1999).

QUOTES

QUOTES

HOW LONG, O LORD?

He who "lives forever" has placed himself at the head of a band of pilgrims who mutter, "How long, O Lord? How long?"

"How long must I endure this sickness?"

"How long must I endure this spouse?"

"How long must I endure this paycheck?"

Do you really want God to answer? He could, you know. He could answer in terms of the here and now with time increments we know. "Two more years on the illness." "The rest of your life in the marriage." "Ten more years for the bills."

But He seldom does that. He usually opts to measure the *here and now* against the *there and then*. And when you compare *this* life to *that* life, this life ain't that long. —Max Lucado, *In the Eye of the Storm* (Nashville, TN: Word Publishing, 1991), p. 118.

God is never so beautiful as through the veil of tears. —Catherine Marshall, quoted in James L. Christensen, *Difficult Funeral Services* (Old Tappan, NJ: Fleming H. Revell, 1985), n.p.

THIS I KNOW

Grief has its rhythm—first, the
Wild swift tide of dark despair,
The time of bleak aloneness
When even God seems not there.

And then, the slow receding—
Till quiet calms the sea,
And bare, unwashed sand everywhere
Where castles used to be.

The gentle lapping of the waves
Upon the shore—and then,
The pearl lined shells of memories
To help us smile again. —Author unknown

THE RELAY RACE

Life is like a relay race, where the baton of values, character, and faith are passed from one generation to another. The runner ahead passes it on, runs by our side for a while, and then we pass it on to those who come after us, one by one. —James L. Christensen, *Difficult Funeral Services* (Old Tappan, NJ: Fleming H. Revell, 1985), n.p.

The tomb is not a blind alley; it is a thoroughfare. It closes on the twilight to open with the dawn. —Victor Hugo

ILLUSTRATIONS

ONE THING FOR SURE

A new mother heard about a wise old man in a nearby Greek village. Seeking counsel on raising her child, she asked the man about the child's future.

"There is one thing I can tell you for sure about your child."

Excitedly, the mother asked, "Oh, what is that?"

The man laid his hand on her shoulder and replied solemnly, "Some day your child will die. There is no exception." —Leith Anderson, "Valley of Death's Shadow," *Preaching Today*, no. 131 (January 1991), audiocassette.

BEAUTY WRAPPED AROUND TROUBLE

What does an oyster do the moment a grain of sand invades its shell? Does it cry out, "Why, with all the other billions of oysters, did this happen to me?" No, it does not complain; it begins the task of wrapping the grain of sand with a milky substance that, by and by, becomes a beautiful pearl. Peter Marshall said, "A pearl is a thing of wonderful beauty wrapped around trouble." —Elmer Towns

I KNOW WHERE HE IS

Trying to explain the sudden death of her grandpa to her little girl, her mother said, "Honey, Grandpa has gone to live with Jesus."

Later, the granddaughter overheard her mother talking on the phone about Grandpa's death. "I lost my father several months ago."

After she hung up the phone, the little girl spoke up, "Mommy, we didn't lose Grandpa. I know where he is." —Michael P. Green, ed., *Illustrations for Biblical Preaching* (Grand Rapids, MI: Baker Book House, 1989), p. 61.

I have learned through my own cancer that in working with the dying, we must be bold. As I lay there nauseated from my treatment, wondering if I would live or die, Christ Himself helped me. That is what people need when they are dying, they need Christ. —Bob Cahall and Dave Hansen, "Cloud of Witnesses," *Leadership Journal* (Winter 1997). http://www.christianity.net/leadership/7L1/7L1105.html (accessed October 4, 1999).

HIT BY A SHADOW

When Donald Barnhouse's wife died, he was left with young daughters to raise alone. While driving to that funeral, which he conducted himself, he wanted to say something to explain all of this to his girls.

They stopped at a traffic light. It was a bright day, and the sun streamed into the car. A truck pulled up next to them, and its shadow darkened the inside of the car. He turned to them and asked whether they would prefer to be hit by the truck or its shadow. They answered: "The shadow can't hurt you."

Quoting Psalm 23, "Even though I walk through the valley of the shadow of death, I will fear no evil, for you are with me," he explained that their mother's death was as if she had been hit by a shadow. It was as if Jesus had stepped in the way in her place. —Leith Anderson, "Valley of Death's Shadow," *Preaching Today*, no. 131 (January 1991), audiocassette.

ILLUSTRATIONS

GOLF STROKE HONORS A FRIEND

Golfer Payne Stewart died tragically in an airplane crash. In the last five years of his life, he had made a deep commitment to Christ, and his faith was well-known in golfing circles.

A fellow Christian golfer memorialized his friend at the next professional golf tournament in Houston. Instead of taking his driver to the first tee, golfer Bob Estes took his putter. Standing over the ball for a few moments, he then putted it about 15 feet.

"That's for Payne," he announced quietly. In a game where each stroke could be worth thousands, Estes voluntarily gave up a stroke in honor of a man who considered his faith and his family more important than a golf score. —*Houston Chronicle,* October 29, 1999, sec. B, p. 2.

CONTRASTING FUNERALS

It's said that during Paul the Apostle's time, heathen funerals were terrifying. The bereaved refused to be comforted, sobbing uncontrollably. In contrast, under the city of Rome, an estimated 300,000 Christians lay buried, victims of Roman persecution. The inscriptions on their tombs: In peace, in sleep, thou livest in God. —Paul Lee Tan, ed., *Resource* (January/February 1991), n.p.

WE WILL SING

At the funeral of a beloved African pastor's wife, great numbers of mourners started a traditional wailing dirge. The pastor suddenly shouted, "Stop! Stop!"
Over the silence of the moment, he plead, "My wife was a child of God. She has gone to be with the Father. We will not cry. We will sing."

The wailing of the mourners soon turned to singing, as the pastor led them in praise to Christ for His victory over death. —James L. Christensen, *Difficult Funeral Services* (Old Tappan, NJ: Fleming H. Revell, 1985), n.p.

USE A FLOWER THE NEXT TIME

Asked to preach my first funeral at age 19, I didn't know what to do. I was thrilled that a senior minister from a neighboring church, who was to assist me with the service, sensed my plight and offered some instructions.

He took me through the minister's manual and pointed out the things I would need to know. Later, I walked out the door to officiate at the funeral of an 82-year-old father of one of my church members.

The funeral proceeded without any problems until we reached the graveside. I knew I was expected to throw some sod onto the casket and pronounce, "Ashes to ashes, dust to dust." Before the committal, I stooped down and picked up a clod of the Georgia clay. It had been hardened by the sun and wouldn't break into pieces. Twisting it in my hand, it still wouldn't break. I prayed silently.

It finally broke into three separate clods in my hand and I valiantly tried to break the clods against the others. In desperation, I dropped the clods onto the casket, one by one. They hit the top of the metal casket with an echoing *thwang*.

Following the committal, the funeral director handed me a flower and told me to squeeze it. Curious, I took the flower and gripped it tightly. "Squeeze it," the director insisted. "Squeeze it until it crushes."

I squeezed the daisy and let the petals fall to the ground.

The director, who had witnessed my embarrassment of dropping the rocks onto the casket at the graveside, said kindly, "Next time, use a flower, not red Georgia clay."

Then he comforted me. "All the family and friends were pulling for you. They like you; you'll be all right."

During the next year, many of the family members came to the church, heard the gospel message and walked forward to receive Jesus Christ as Savior. —Elmer Towns

SHE TURNED TO A NAZARENE CARPENTER

At a prayer breakfast, then Vice President George Bush told of a trip to Russia. He was there to represent the United States at the funeral of Leonid Brezhnev. He said the funeral was precise and stoic. No tears were shed and no emotion was shown.

There was one exception. Mrs. Brezhnev was the last to witness the body before the coffin was closed. She stood by its side for a few moments, and then reached down to perform the sign of the cross on her husband's chest.

In the hour of death, she went not to Lenin, not to Karl Marx, not to Krushchev. She turned to a Nazarene carpenter who had lived two thousand years ago and who dared to claim: Don't let your hearts be troubled. Trust in God, and trust in me. —Max Lucado, *A Gentle Thunder* (Dallas: Word Publishing, 1995), p. 64.

LET IT GO

Ralph Waldo Emerson was confronted by a lady after one of his lectures. "Dr. Emerson, don't you know the world is coming to an end!"

He replied gently, "Oh, well, let it go. We can get along without it." —James L. Christensen, *Difficult Funeral Services* (Old Tappan, NJ: Fleming H. Revell, 1985), n.p.

DEATH DOESN'T HAVE A GOOD TRACK RECORD

In the cartoon, *Shoe*, Skyler holds up his report card and says, "I study all night and get a lousy C. And dumb Lenny lucks out an A!"

His father replies, "You may as well get used to it, Skyler, life isn't fair. But then, death doesn't have a good track record either." —Jeff MacNelly, creator of *Shoe*®

WEDDINGS

However, each one of you also must love his wife as he loves himself, and the wife must respect her husband. Ephesians 5:33

The idea of marriage goes back to Genesis 2, when God united Adam and Eve and made them "one flesh" (Genesis 2:24). The Garden of Eden was the location of the first marriage; the Lord was the first to officiate. From the beginning of time until now, the institution of marriage has continued through all races and cultures. The uniting in marriage of one man and one woman was God's plan from the very beginning.

While the concept of marriage came from God, our society has added various wedding traditions according to its culture and preferences. Many of our current wedding traditions arise out of ancient customs. For example, the throwing of rice was thought to promote fertility,[1] the bridal attendants and herbs in the bridal bouquet were thought to ward off evil spirits,[2] and the receiving line was thought to promote good luck for all of the guests who touched the happy couple.[3]

The marriage metaphor is alive throughout the New Testament. Believers in Christ are referred to as the Bride and Christ is called the Bridegroom. A great marriage supper will celebrate the victory that Christ has won through His victorious life, crucifixion and resurrection. Both the preparation and the wedding ceremony itself are great ministry opportunities for the church.

A WEDDING CEREMONY

WEDDING

OPENING REMARKS

Pastor: In the beginning days of creation, God was pleased with all He had created. Looking at Adam's solitude, however, He realized that humankind needed companionship, and woman came into existence. In the innocence of Eden the marriage relationship began! God initiated this relationship because of our need for support, care and love. Over the centuries, countless couples have searched for acceptance, love and companionship in the womb of marriage.

Today we gather to celebrate these characteristics in the marriage of *(groom's name)* and *(bride's name).* This marriage event is in one sense a very private time for *(groom's name)* and *(bride's name),* yet it publicly speaks to everyone that *(groom's name)* and *(bride's name)* belong uniquely to each other with no one intruding upon their relationship.

To this end we may declare with the psalmist, "I will give thanks to the Lord with my whole heart; I will tell of all thy wonderful deeds" (Psalm 9:1 *RSV).*

Pastor: *(To the bride's father)* Who gives this woman to be married to this man?

Father: Her family lovingly gives her to this man for a lifetime of commitment.

Pastor: If you desire your life to be touched with eternal beauty, then catch and cherish the days of your courtship. Even when immersed in the commonplace experiences ahead, refuse steadfastly to allow your vision to be blurred.

God's Word declares that love, joy, hope and goodness should be practiced by all. But in no place is it better to be practiced than in the home. Becoming a husband or a wife does not destroy your individuality; rather it enhances and enriches your natural skills, abilities and talents. God will help you grow and develop as people planned in His image. As you contribute your best to one another, you will become one in life's most intimate and fulfilling relationships.

This is our prayer as we witness the beginning of your life's journey together.

Friend: Let us pray *(extemporaneous or written prayer by a friend of either groom or bride).*

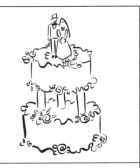

WEDDING

GIVING OF RINGS

Pastor:	What do you give as a token of your love and commitment to one another?
Couple:	A ring (*best man and matron/maid of honor give rings to pastor, who then hands rings to couple*).
Pastor	(*To groom*) Place the ring on (*bride's name*) finger and repeat after me.
Groom:	I, (*groom's name*), give you this ring, (*bride's name*), . . . out of sincere commitment. . . . I know this ring is only a symbol . . . but a lasting symbol of my love.
Bride:	I, (*bride's name*), receive this ring, (*groom's name*), as your symbol of lasting love.
Pastor	(*To bride*) Place this ring on (*groom's name*) finger and repeat after me.
Bride:	I, (*bride's name*), give you this ring, (*groom's name*), . . . out of sincere commitment. . . . I know this ring is only a symbol . . . but a lasting symbol of my love.
Groom:	I, (*groom's name*), receive this ring, (*bride's name*), as your symbol of lasting love.

SPECIAL MUSIC: "WITH THIS RING"

(Words and music by Clyde Otis and Vincent Corso, *Hudson Bay Music, Inc.*)

VOWS

Pastor:	Benjamin Franklin has been credited with the comment, "It is the man and woman united that made the complete human being. Together, they are most likely to succeed in the world."
	It is with this thought of unity that you come now to take your vows.
Pastor:	(*Groom's name*), repeat after me:
Groom:	I, (*groom's name*), take you, (*bride's name*), to be my wife . . . now and throughout the rest of our lives. . . . I pledge my undying faithfulness . . . and will continue to love you always.
Pastor:	(*Bride's name*), repeat after me:
Bride:	I, (*bride's name*), take you, (*groom's name*), to be my husband . . . now and throughout the rest of our lives. . . . I pledge my undying faithfulness . . . and will continue to love you always.

SPECIAL MUSIC: "LOVE WILL BE OUR HOME"

(Words and music by Steven Curtis Chapman, *Contemporary Christian Wedding Songbook*, Milwaukee, WI: Hal Leonard Corporation, 1995).

ANNOUNCEMENT OF NEW COUPLE

Pastor: *(Groom's name)* and *(bride's name)*, it is now my joy, granted me by the State of *(the name of the state)* and *(church name)*, to declare to all that you are husband and wife, since you have of your free will given commitments to one another. I charge you to become one in your relationship. *(Groom's name)*, you may now kiss your bride!

Pastor: Friends, it is my pleasure to introduce to you Mr. and Mrs. *(groom's last name)*.

WEDDING

69

QUOTES

QUOTES

Hear the mellow wedding bells,
Golden bells!
What a world of happiness
Their harmony foretells! —Edgar Allan Poe, "The Bells"

Two such as you with
such a master speed
Cannot be parted
nor be swept away
From one another
once you are agreed
That life is only
Life forevermore
Together
Wing to wing
And oar to oar —Robert Frost, from "The Master Speed"

My most brilliant achievement was my ability to persuade my wife to marry me. —Winston Churchill

Marriage is the fusion of two hearts—the union of two lives—the coming together of two tributaries. —Peter Marshall

You will reciprocally promise love,
loyalty and matrimonial honesty.
We only want for you this day
that these words would constitute
the principle of your entire life;
and that with the help
of the divine grace
you will observe these solemn vows
that today, before God,
you formulate. —Author unknown

ILLUSTRATIONS

BETTER OFFER

During the wedding rehearsal, the groom approached the pastor with an unusual offer: "Look, I'll give you $100 if you'll change the wedding vows. When you get to me and the part where I'm to promise to 'love, honor and obey,' I'd appreciate it if you'd just leave that part out." He passed the minister a $100 bill and walked away, satisfied.

The big day came, and the bride and groom were exchanging their vows. When it came time for the groom's vows, the pastor looked the young man in the eye and said: "Will you promise to kneel before her, obey her every command and wish, serve her breakfast in bed every morning of your life and swear eternally before God and your lovely wife that you will not ever even look at another woman, as long as you both shall live?"

The groom gulped, looked around, and said in a tiny voice, "Yes." Then the groom leaned toward the pastor and hissed, "I thought we had a deal."

The pastor put the $100 bill into the groom's hand and whispered back, "She made me a much better offer." —Elmer Towns

RULES FOR A HAPPY MARRIAGE

- Never let both partners be angry at once.
- Never yell at each other unless the house is on fire.
- Yield to the wishes of the other as an exercise in self-discipline if you can't think of a better reason.
- If you have a choice between making yourself or your mate look good, choose your mate.
- If you have any criticism, make it lovingly.
- Never bring up a mistake of the past.
- Neglect the whole world rather than each other.
- Never let the day end without saying at least one kind or complimentary thing to your life's partner.
- Never meet without an affectionate welcome.
- Never let the sun go down on an argument unresolved.
- When you do wrong, make sure you have talked it out and asked for forgiveness.
- Remember that in a quarrel, the one with the least sense will be talking most. —Dr. Laura Schlessinger, *Dr. Laura.com*. http://www.drlaura.com/funfaxes.html (accessed June 1997).

71

Section Two

~

COMMEMORATIVE EVENTS

FATHER'S DAY

IT STARTED WITH GRATITUDE

A father to the fatherless, a defender of widows, is God in his holy dwelling. Psalm 68:5

When Jesus taught us to pray, He began with the expression of reverence and adoration, "Our Father." The relationship He had with His heavenly Father serves as a model for all family relationships—love, respect, obedience, dependence. Earthly fathers serve as His ambassadors to their families. And the respect we bestow on them is, in effect, ultimately bestowed on our heavenly Father.

Like Mother's Day, the idea of Father's Day originated from a grateful daughter. Mrs. Sonora Smart Dodd of Spokane, Washington, proposed the idea of the holiday in grateful memory of her own devoted father.[1] Her father, Henry Jackson Smart, had raised her and her five siblings as a single parent after the death of their mother. Mr. Smart's birthday fell on June 19, and his daughter proposed this as the fitting date of commemoration.[2]

Mrs. Dodd first publicized her idea in 1909, and various American presidents supported the idea. In 1926, a National Father's Day Committee was formed in New York City to promote the event. Thirty years later, Congress officially recognized Father's Day as a national holiday. However, it wasn't until 1972 that President Richard Nixon established a permanent national observance of Father's Day on the third Sunday in June.[3]

SERMON SKETCH

REMEMBERING FATHERHOOD —ELMER TOWNS

MAIN TEXT: EXODUS 20:12

Honor your father and your mother, so that you may live long in the land the LORD your God is giving you.

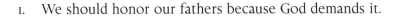

1. We should honor our fathers because God demands it.

    For God said, "Honor your father and mother" and "Anyone who curses his father or mother must be put to death" (Matthew 15:4).

2. We should respect our fathers because of their heavenly origin.

    Our Father in heaven (Matthew 6:9).

3. We should obey our fathers because accountability requires it.

    Rise in the presence of the aged, show respect for the elderly and revere your God. I am the LORD (Leviticus 19:32).

    Anyone who attacks his father or his mother must be put to death (Exodus 21:15).

FATHER ABRAHAM —JERRY BRECHEISEN

TEXT: GENESIS 22:1-18

1. Abraham listened to God.

    Some time later God tested Abraham. He said to him, "Abraham!" "Here I am," he replied (v. 1).

    But the angel of the LORD called out to him from heaven, "Abraham! Abraham!" "Here I am," he replied (v. 11).

2. Abraham obeyed God.

    Early the next morning Abraham got up and saddled his donkey. He took with him two of his servants and his son Isaac. When he had cut enough wood for the burnt offering, he set out for the place God had told him about (vv. 3,4).

3. Abraham believed God.

    He said to his servants, "Stay here with the donkey while I and the boy go over there. We will worship and then we will come back to you" (v. 5).

    Abraham answered, "God himself will provide the lamb for the burnt offering, my son." And the two of them went on together (v. 8).

QUOTES

A man never knows how to be a son until he becomes a father. By the time a man realizes that maybe his father was right, he usually has a son who thinks he's wrong. —Albert Wells, Jr., ed., *Inspiring Quotations* (Nashville, TN: Thomas Nelson, 1988), p. 72.

While I don't minimize the vital role played by a mother, I believe a successful family begins with her husband. —James Dobson, quoted in *Inspiring Quotations*, ed. Albert Wells, Jr. (Nashville, TN: Thomas Nelson, 1988), p. 71.

One of the best ways to correct your children is to correct the example you are setting for them. —Author unknown

It is easier to build boys than to mend men. —Albert Wells, Jr., ed., *Inspiring Quotations* (Nashville, TN: Thomas Nelson, 1988), n.p.

If God's character is to be understood in terms of my life (as a father), what does my child think of God? —Lee Haines, quoted in *Inspiring Quotations*, ed. Albert Wells, Jr. (Nashville, TN: Thomas Nelson, 1988), p. 71.

QUOTES

ILLUSTRATIONS

ILLUSTRATIONS

BACKACHE OR HEARTACHE?

After a hard day's work a construction worker was seen playing catch with his son. His friend stopped in. "Playing catch?" he commented. "I should think physical activity would be the last thing on your mind after a long day."

The father replied, "It's a matter of choice. I'd rather have a backache now than a heartache later." —Herman Turner, quoted in *Speaker's Illustrations for Special Days*, ed. Charles L. Wallis (New York: Abingdon Press, 1956), n.p.

GOD CREATED ALL THIS

A father was trying to explain the Creation to his son as they walked through the woods, "Son, God made all of this—every single leaf, on every single tree."

"Yeah, I know, Dad," the boy responded excitedly. "And He did it all with His left hand!"

"With His left hand?" the father asked. "Where did you ever hear that?"

"Last Sunday, my Sunday School teacher read from the Bible and it said that Jesus was sitting on His Father's right hand." —Author unknown

HALL-OF-FAMER

Workers remodeling the Baseball Hall of Fame discovered a photograph in the crevice of a display case. It was the photo of a minor league baseball player dressed in his uniform. It had an inscription stapled to it.

"Dad, you were always there for us. You were a true Hall-of-Famer."

Who put it there? A custodian? A Hall of Fame worker? No one knows. But one thing is known: It was placed there by a son whose father had made a difference in his life. —King Duncan, ed., *Dynamic Illustrations* (April/May/June, 1999), n.p.

HOW OLD IS DADDY?

Sitting around the dinner table, the discussion turned to Daddy's age. "I know how old he is!" the youngest member of the family announced.

"How old do you think he is?" Mom asked.

"He's 32," the little brother replied.

"And how do you know that?" his mother asked.

Stirring the vegetables on his plate, he answered, "Mom, remember when you were folding clothes the other day? Well, his age was on his underwear." —Elmer Towns

LOOK FOR THE GOLD

Andrew Carnegie on developing people: "You develop people in the same way you mine for gold. When you mine for gold, you move tons of dirt to find a single ounce of gold. However, you don't look for the dirt—you look for the gold." —Paul Lee Tan, ed., *Resource* (March/April 1991), n.p.

LOOKS AREN'T EVERYTHING

Looking very solemn, the doctor motioned for the wife of his patient to meet him outside the examining room.

"I'll have to say, your husband just doesn't look good to me."

"Me either," she responded, "but looks aren't everything. And besides, that, he's a good father." —Cal and Rose Samra, eds., *Holy Humor, Inspirational Wit and Cartoons* (Nashville, TN: Thomas Nelson, 1997), n.p.

PUT AWAY CHILDISH THINGS

Dad came home from work and tried to put the car in the garage. Before he could get to the garage, he had to clean out the driveway. First, he put the bike aside; then the basketball; next the inline skates; then the baseball bat and then the remote control race car.

Greeting his wife at the door, he said, "You know, honey, now I know what that Scripture verse means, "When I became a man, I put away childish things." —Michael P. Green, ed., *Illustrations for Biblical Preaching* (Grand Rapids, MI: Baker Book House, 1989), n.p.

WHEN YOU GROW UP

"Son, what will you be doing when you grow up and become as big as your father?" a father asked philosophically.

His little boy replied quickly, "Dieting!" —Jerry Brecheisen

WHAT DOES DAD HAVE TO DO WITH IT?

Two daughters were having a discussion about family resemblance. "I look like Mom," said my nine-year-old, "but I have Dad's eyes and Dad's lips."

The six-year-old said, "And I look just like Dad, but I have light hair." Then she turned to me. "Mom," she asked, "what does Dad have to do with us being born anyway?"

Her older sister jumped right in. "Don't be stupid, Christina. Dad is the one who drove Mom to the hospital." —Kathleen O'Neill, quoted in *Reader's Digest* (June 1996), p. 103.

THE COST IS WORTH IT

Two fathers were discussing the cost of raising children. "I know the costs are great, but it's worth it to me just to have someone in the house who knows how to operate our computer." —Jerry Brecheisen

THE BIBLE STORY QUESTION

A father was reading a Bible story to his young son. Reading about God's warning to Lot to flee the city and not turn back, he was suddenly interrupted.

"Dad, whatever happened to the flea?" —Mark Hollingsworth

GO HOME AT ONCE!

The noted psychologist, Karl Menninger, was asked by a father who was attending his lecture, "When should we begin teaching values to our child?"

Menninger asked, "And how old is the child?"

"Three and a half," the father replied.

"Then, go home at once!" Menninger advised. —Robert R. Kopp, "Mother's Day/Father's Day," *The Abingdon Preaching Annual 1996*, ed. Michael Duduit (Nashville, TN: Abingdon Press, 1995), p. 42.

YOU DIDN'T ASK YOUR DAD TO HELP

A little boy struggled with a big rock that someone had mischievously placed in his sandbox. Since it stood in the way of the "freeway" that he was constructing in the sand, it had to be removed.

He dug around the rock and loosened it. He tried to lift it but he couldn't. He laid down in the sand and tried to push it with his feet. It wouldn't budge.

The little boy's dad noticed the effort and came over to the sandbox. "What's the problem, son?"

"Daddy, I've tried everything to get this big rock out of the sandbox," the boy replied tearfully.

"No, I'm afraid you haven't tried everything."

"What do you mean, Daddy?"

The dad reached down and picked up the rock, "You didn't ask your dad to help." —Wayne Rice, *Hot Illustrations for Youth* (El Cajon, CA: Youth Specialties, 1994), n.p.

WELL-ADJUSTED CHILDREN

A positive and continuous relationship to one's father has been found to be associated with a good self-concept, higher self-esteem, higher self-confidence in personal and social interaction, higher moral maturity, reduced rates of unwed teen pregnancy, greater internal control and higher career aspirations. Fathers who are affectionate, nurturing and actively involved in child-rearing are more likely to have well-adjusted children. —Dr. George Rekers, *Homemade*, vol. 11, no. 1 (1987), n.p.

ILLUSTRATIONS

THE SAFEST PLACE TO STAND

Max Lucado tells of speaking at a funeral of a family friend. The friend's son told of an incident when a tornado hit their small town.

His father hustled the kids indoors and had them lie under a mattress. The son remembered peeking out from under the mattress and seeing his father standing by a window, watching the funnel cloud.

When the young boy saw his father, he crawled out from under the mattress, and ran to wrap his arms around his dad's leg.

"Something told me," he said, "that the safest place to stand in a storm was next to my father." —Max Lucado, *In the Eye of the Storm* (Dallas: Word Publishing, 1991), n.p.

ONLY ONE THING MATTERED

Entering the parsonage at the end of a full and hectic Sunday, the phone rang. It was a disgruntled church member calling to register a complaint about the building program. For the next 30 minutes she took me to task on every facet of ministry.

Upstairs, my wife was giving our 18-month-old son his evening bath. As the lady droned on, I heard my wife say, "Seth Aaron Toler, come back here!"

Naked and sliding down the stairs head first, he was soon in my lap. Bath water covered my suit as he shivered and shook his curly blond head. He hugged me, and kissed me on each cheek. "Daddy," he said, "I wuv you!"

Tears streamed down my cheeks, as the caller finalized her Sunday evening fireside chat. In that moment, only one thing mattered. I knew I was loved. God was not late when I needed encouragement! —Stan Toler

ILLUSTRATIONS

KENNEDY FAMILY DINNER

In *The Kennedy Women*, Pearl Buck says the Kennedy family had a full family dinner served at the main dining table on evenings when the father, Joseph Kennedy, was home.

Presiding at the head of the table, the father strictly enforced ground rules on conversation. They never talked about money. They never criticized another Kennedy. And finally, they were urged to talk about issues and ideas, particularly political issues and ideas.

Sometimes the ambassador assigned the children homework that prepared them for the next family discussion. This kind of family dining may be far too structured for most families. But teaching the children to talk about ideas and issues apparently paid off. —Leslie Parrott, *The Habit of Happiness* (Waco, TX: Word Publishing, 1987), p. 85.

JUST LIKE YOU

A man and his wife came home from a night out. The baby-sitter answered the door and the father inquired how things went. The baby-sitter replied, "Well, pretty good, but I think you'll need to have a little talk with your son." Soon, the little three-year-old boy peeked around the corner. His head was completely shaven.

"What on earth have you done to your head?" the father exclaimed.

"I shaved it with your electric razor, Dad."

"And why did you do that?" the father replied sternly.

The little boy pointed to his father's bald head and explained, "Because I wanted to be just like you!" —Author unknown

AD-LIBBED

In the comic strip *Calvin and Hobbes*, six-year-old Calvin's home has been broken into and robbed.

His parents try to sleep and the wife says, "Are you still awake, too?"

The husband answered, "I was just thinking. It's funny. When I was a kid, I thought grownups never worried about anything. I trusted my parents to take care of everything, and it never occurred to me that they might not know how. I figured that once you grew up, you automatically knew what to do in any given scenario. I don't think I'd have been in such a hurry to reach adulthood if I'd known the whole thing was going to be ad-libbed." —Bill Watterson, creator of *Calvin and Hobbes*®

LIGHT AND LOVE

Thomas Kinkade is one of the most popular contemporary artists in the world. His paintings, their prints and reproductions sell more than any other artists' in the world and have won numerous prestigious art awards.

Kinkade is a master of luminism, a school of art that paints in such a way as to bring out the natural reflection of light in the paint. This method gives his works an otherworldly "glow." Though this method makes for beautiful art, that is not Kinkade's primary reason for using it. Thomas Kinkade, a lifelong Christian, wants his work to bring to mind "the light of the world," Jesus Christ.

Hundreds of people write to Thomas Kinkade to tell him how his paintings have lifted them out of sadness or drew them closer to God. Some have been saved from suicide or become Christians through viewing his art.

Kinkade is married to his childhood sweetheart, Nanette, and the two of them have three daughters. Though his own parents were divorced, Thomas learned through the church how to have a strong, faith-filled marriage. He cherishes his family relationships, and it shows in his art. In every painting he creates, Thomas Kinkade hides the initials of his wife and three daughters. —Mario M. Schalesky, "The Nazarene Church Sparks the Painter of Light," *Herald of Holiness* (May 1997), pp. 22-25, 32.

ILLUSTRATIONS

THE SHINY DOORS

An Amish boy and his father visited a large mall. They noticed a wall with two shiny doors that opened and shut.

"What's that, Father?" the boy asked, not having seen an elevator before.

His father answered, "Son, I don't know. Let's watch."

As they sat on a bench near the elevator, an elderly lady walked up to the doors and pressed a nearby button. The doors opened and she walked through.

The boy and his father watched as the some lights lit up, and a bell sounded.

Soon, the shiny doors opened and a beautiful young woman emerged.

Without taking his eyes off the young woman, he patted his son's arm. "Son, go fetch your ma. Maybe she'd like to go through those doors." —Author unknown

GOT FAMILY?

An Amish buggy driver cracked the whip at a horsefly buzzing over the horse's back. It expired suddenly. His son was riding with him. "Nice shot, Father!" Another horsefly hovered, and another crack of the whip. The results were the same.

Suddenly a wasp approached. The Amish man did nothing.

"Father?" the boy wondered, "Why didst thou not crack thy whip?"

"Because, my son," the buggy driver said soberly, "he's got family nearby."
—Charles L. Wallis, ed., *Speaker's Illustrations for Special Days* (New York: Abingdon Press, 1956), p. 34.

ILLUSTRATIONS

A SPECIAL PRAYER REQUEST

A little boy was having trouble behaving in church.

Finally, the exasperated father picked him up, threw him over his shoulder and marched down the center aisle.

Knowing what would happen when they reached the foyer, the little boy raised his hand and shouted to the audience, "Folks, I have a special prayer request!" —*The Executive Speechwriters Newsletter*

GRADUATION

Give everyone what you owe . . . if honor, then honor. Romans 13:7

The apostle Paul encouraged believers to celebrate the achievements of others. Whether in a personal word or in a public ceremony, the church is serving its Master when it extends its hand of support and brotherly love. If it is called to "train up a child," then it is only right to acknowledge the steps toward completion.

Many churches choose to recognize recent graduates of high school, college and graduate school. This does not replace the traditional baccalaureate service; it is simply recognition within the church family that a student has successfully completed a new level of education. Some churches incorporate an entire Graduation Sunday into their calendars and use the day not only to congratulate the students' accomplishments but also to promote children from one grade of Sunday School to the next.

During the church ceremony, ministers may award the graduate with a Bible or other small gift. A short exhortation to follow Christ and to trust Him for the future is also appropriate, and a prayer of blessing usually follows. Graduates are often encouraged to wear their ornamental caps and gowns. Families tend to view the recognition of graduates in the church service as a symbol of blessing and dedication to the Lord.

SERMON
SKETCHES

SERMON SKETCH

STRENGTH IN A STRANGE LAND —ELMER TOWNS

TEXT: DANIEL 1

A. Introduction

You are about to enter a whole new world. There are four lessons from the life of Daniel that will give you strength for your journey.

1. God is in control.
2. There is power in a purpose.
3. You must face the challenge to be *in* the world, but not *of* the world.
4. God is faithful.

B. Conclusion

Anything less than God will let you down. — *Stanley Jones*

GIVE ME THIS MOUNTIAN —STAN TOLER

MAIN TEXT: NUMBERS 23:3,4

Then Balaam said to Balak, "Stay here beside your offering while I go aside. Perhaps the LORD will come to meet with me. Whatever he reveals to me I will tell you." Then he went off to a barren height. God met with him, and Balaam said, "I have prepared seven altars, and on each altar I have offered a bull and a ram."

1. The Mountain of Learning
2. The Mountain of Commitment
3. The Mountain of Change
4. The Mountain of Peer Pressure

After this I looked, and there before me was a door standing open in heaven. And the voice I had first heard speaking to me like a trumpet said, "Come up here, and I will show you what must take place after this" Revelation 4:1.

86

QUOTES

A child enters your home and it's noisy for the next eighteen years. Then the child leaves for college and the silence is deafening. —J. A. Holmes

Life is no brief candle to me. It is a splendid torch which I have got hold of for the moment, and I want to make it burn as brightly as possible before handing it on to future generations. —George Bernard Shaw

I believe in college because it takes kids away from home at the point when they start asking questions. —Will Rogers, quoted in *Dynamic Illustrations*, ed. King Duncan (July/August/September 1999), p. 14.

About the time we're ready to graduate from the school of experience, somebody adds one more class. —Author unknown

ILLUSTRATIONS

ILLUSTRATIONS

BUILDING A PLACE IN THE HEART

William Rockefeller, brother of John D. Rockefeller, announced that he was going to build a tomb for himself that would cost over a quarter of a million dollars.

A writer in *Forbes* magazine commented, "Few men of his wealth and opportunities have more completely failed to build for themselves a worthy place in the hearts of their fellow men." —David W. Richardson, quoted in *The Abingdon Preacher's Annual 1994*, ed. John K. Bergland (Nashville, TN: Abingdon Press, 1993), p. 38.

FRESHMAN DREAMS

It was Parent's Day at State College. Some of the parents had gathered in the coffee shop. One remarked, "I'm sure you have so many dreams for that freshman son of yours!"

His mother replied, "Yes, of course. For several years now, we've been dreaming of the day he becomes a sophomore." —King Duncan, ed., *Dynamic Illustrations* (July/August/September 1999), p. 18.

KEEP YOUR EYES ON THE ROAD

Our generation is like the man who was riding his motorcycle on a warm summer day when he had an accident.

Since it was a sunny day and the road was very straight, the police officer asked him what happened.

He replied, "I was watching the light poles along the highway."

The man was so mesmerized by the light poles that he missed a sharp turn in the road. Since the light poles continued in a straight line despite the curve in the road, so did the motorcycle rider. —William H. Hinson, *The Power of Holy Habits* (Nashville, TN: Abingdon Press, 1991), p. 63.

PLANNED NEGLECT

A famed concert pianist was asked how she had become such a virtuoso. She replied, "Planned neglect." Everything else had been sacrificed to meet her goal of being a pianist. —Michael P. Green, ed., *Illustrations for Biblical Preaching* (Grand Rapids, MI: Baker Book House, 1989), p. 51.

88

THE ONLY ONE WITH THE ANSWER

Johnny came home from school crying. "What on earth is wrong?" his mother inquired.

"The teacher asked a question in school today, and I was the only one who could answer it," he sobbed.

"Honey, why would that make you sad? I should think you would be proud," his mother remarked. "What was the question?"

Johnny brushed the tears, "Who put the Super Glue® on my chair?!" —Joel Goodman, ed., *Laughing Matters*, vol. 4, no. 3 (1995), n.p.

GLOW ALL THE TIME

Bart Starr reminisced about his beloved coach, Vince Lomardi: "To win, you have to have a certain amount of mental toughness. Coach Lombardi gave me that. He taught me that you must have a flaming desire to win. It's got to dominate all your waking hours. It can't ever wane. It's got to glow in you all the time." —Jerry Kramer, ed., *Lombardi . . . Winning Is the Only Thing* (New York: World Publishing, 1970), p. 86.

READY WITH THE ANSWERS

When I first entered Bible college, I began memorizing Scripture for my personal growth and to answer my questions about my faith. I thought if I had answers for my questions from God's Word, I would have answers for others. The Bible exhorts us to be ready with "an answer to everyone who asks you to give the reason for the hope that you have" (1 Peter 3:15). —Elmer Towns

ILLUSTRATIONS

89

INDEPENDENCE DAY

Blessed is the nation whose God is the LORD, the people he chose for his inheritance.
Psalm 33:12

Independence Day is the main national holiday of the United States. On this day, we celebrate the freedom that so uniquely characterizes America. It is a day dedicated to the memory of the political leaders and military men who sacrificed their time and life for the sake of freedom. It is also a day to recognize a national dependence upon God. The church has a unique opportunity to call attention to both—the independence of the nation and its dependence upon its God.

In 1776, the United States consisted of thirteen colonies that were struggling to find freedom from tyrannical British rule. The British were levying heavy taxes on the Americans, and there was growing unrest among the colonists. However, England's King George III ignored the indignant colonists and continued legislating taxes without the colonists' representation in Parliament.[1]

The hard feelings built, and the colonists established a Continental Congress of their own. For a year, delegates to the Continental Congress worked with England in an attempt to reconcile differences. Attempts to make peace, however, soon proved futile. Thomas Jefferson, John Adams, Benjamin Franklin and others participated in drafting a statement of independence from Britain. King George was not interested in reconciliation, and on July 4, 1776, nine of the thirteen colonies signed a Declaration of Independence. War began—and so did American liberty.[2]

Canada celebrates Canada Day on July 1, marking "the anniversary of the unification of Upper and Lower Canada (what are now Ontario and Quebec), New Brunswick and Nova Scotia as the Dominion of Canada. This union became effective by the passage of the British North America Act, on July 1, 1867.

Prior to a constitutional revision in 1982, Canada Day was known as Dominion Day. The day is marked throughout Canada by parades, fireworks, and the display of flags.[3]

SERMON SKETCH

SAINTLY CITIZENS —JERRY BRECHEISEN

MAIN TEXT: ROMANS 13:1-14

1. Respect the leaders of the land.

Everyone must submit himself to the governing authorities, for there is no authority except that which God has established. The authorities that exist have been established by God. Consequently, he who rebels against the authority is rebelling against what God has instituted, and those who do so will bring judgment on themselves. For rulers hold no terror for those who do right, but for those who do wrong. Do you want to be free from fear of the one in authority? Then do what is right and he will commend you. For he is God's servant to do you good. But if you do wrong, be afraid, for he does not bear the sword for nothing. He is God's servant, an agent of wrath to bring punishment on the wrongdoer. Therefore, it is necessary to submit to the authorities, not only because of possible punishment but also because of conscience (vv.1-5).

2. Obey the laws of the land.

This is also why you pay taxes, for the authorities are God's servants, who give their full time to governing. Give everyone what you owe him: If you owe taxes, pay taxes; if revenue, then revenue; if respect, then respect; if honor, then honor. Let no debt remain outstanding, except the continuing debt to love one another, for he who loves his fellowman has fulfilled the law (vv. 6-8).

3. Contribute to the spiritual welfare of the land.

The commandments, "Do not commit adultery," "Do not murder," "Do not steal," "Do not covet," and whatever other commandment there may be, are summed up in this one rule: "Love your neighbor as yourself." Love does no harm to its neighbor. Therefore love is the fulfillment of the law. And do this, understanding the present time. The hour has come for you to wake up from your slumber, because our salvation is nearer now than when we first believed. The night is nearly over; the day is almost here. So let us put aside the deeds of darkness and put on the armor of light. Let us behave decently, as in the daytime, not in orgies and drunkenness, not in sexual immorality and debauchery, not in dissension and jealousy. Rather, clothe yourselves with the Lord Jesus Christ, and do not think about how to gratify the desires of the sinful nature (vv. 9-14).

QUOTES

The choice before us is plain: Christ or chaos, conviction or compromise, discipline or disintegration. I am rather tired of hearing about our rights and privileges as American citizens. The time is come—it is now—when we ought to hear about the duties and responsibilities of our citizenship. America's future depends upon her accepting and demonstrating God's government. —Peter Marshall, quoted in *America's God and Country Encyclopedia of Quotations* (Dallas: Fame Publishing, 1996), n.p.

Reading about the mishaps suffered on the Fourth of July, Will Rogers commented, "We've killed more people celebrating our independence than we lost fighting for it." —Angela Akers and King Duncan, eds., *Amusing Grace* (Knoxville, TN: Seven Worlds Corporation, 1993), n.p.

As ministers, a great responsibility rests upon us as leaders. We cannot expect our people to register and become citizens until we as leaders set the standard. —Martin Luther King, Jr.

With their feet on the ground and their eyes on the stars, grassroots leaders everywhere are busy shaping the next American century around the conviction that liberty is a gift from God, not government. Because they know that one man or woman, fired by an idea and free to pursue his or her dreams, can make history, even while making a profit. —Gerald R. Ford, quoted in *Rediscovering American Values: The Foundations of Our Freedom for the 21st Century*, ed. Dick De Vos (New York: Plume Printing, 1997), n.p.

THE LOVE OF LIBERTY

Our reliance is in the love of liberty which God has planted in us. Our defense is in the spirit which prized liberty as the heritage of all men, in all lands everywhere. Destroy this spirit and you have planted the seeds of despotism at your own doors. Familiarize yourselves with the chains of bondage and you prepare your own limbs to wear them. Accustomed to trample on the rights of others, you have lost the genius of your own independence and become the fit subjects of the first cunning tyrant who rises among you. —Abraham Lincoln, quoted in *The Pastor's Weekly Briefing*, vol. 6, no. 27 (July 3, 1998), n.p.

QUOTES

93

QUOTES

THE GENIUS OF OUR SOCIETY

The genius of our society is that we've included biblical principles, yet have established no national religion. It is not an amoral system for it understands itself to be "under God," yet allows for freedom of and even indifference to religion. —Frank Lyman, quoted in *Dynamic Illustrations*, ed. King Duncan (July/August/September 1999), n.p.

ILLUSTRATIONS

WHAT IS THE NAME OF OUR COUNTRY?

The first grade teacher pointed to the American flag, "What flag is this?"

One of the students replied enthusiastically, "That's our country's flag!"

"And what is the name of our country?" the teacher asked.

The student quickly replied, "'Tis of thee." —King Duncan, ed., *Dynamic Illustrations* (July/August/September 1999), n.p.

THE PAINTING

In 1989, a financial analyst from Philadelphia paid $4 for a painting at a sale. He didn't care for the painting but liked the frame.

Taking the picture apart, a copy of the Declaration of Independence, about the size of a business envelope, fell out. Years later, he showed it to a friend who encouraged him to have it appraised.

He discovered that hours after finishing work on the Declaration in 1776, the Continental Congress had delivered a handwritten draft to a printer with orders to distribute copies to several state assemblies, conventions, and army officers for display.

Only 24 of the original printings have survived. The one in the picture frame was in mint condition and was sold at a 1991 auction for $2.4 million. —King Duncan, ed., *Dynamic Illustrations* (July/August/September 1999), n.p.

THE PATRIOTIC SERVICE

A family not accustomed to attending church visited a local church on a Fourth of July weekend. The entire service focused on patriotism.

After the call to worship and the invocation, the worship leader led the congregation in singing the national anthem.

At end of the last chorus, the family's four-year-old son suddenly shouted, "Play ball!" —Cal and Rose Samra, eds., *More Holy Humor* (Nashville, TN: Thomas Nelson, 1997), p. 41.

LABOR DAY

Six days you shall labor and do all your work. Deuteronomy 5:13

Since the time of Adam, labor has been a part of God's economy. God grants each of us six days to utilize the intellectual and physical abilities that He has given us for the betterment of society and the welfare of our homes and families.

In 1882, the United States celebrated its first Labor Day.[1] Today we usually view Labor Day as an extra holiday—an extension of summer. But when the holiday was created over a hundred years ago, its purpose was quite different.

The middle of the Industrial Revolution, 1882 was a year of labor struggles. Although we don't know which of several men organized the first Labor Day, we do know that it was first observed on Tuesday, September 5, 1882, in New York City.[2] It was promoted by the Central Labor Union for the purpose of political protest against current working conditions.[3] In 1884, the Central Labor Union chose the first Monday in September as the official date of the holiday, and other large cities began to follow suit. By 1885, many industrial centers celebrated Labor Day. Nine years later, Congress voted to make the day a legal holiday in the District of Columbia and in the territories.[4]

Today, some celebrate Labor Day by attending citywide parades, others gather at parks for end-of-summer barbecues and still others celebrate by simply relaxing quietly at home.

SERMON SKETCHES

YOUR LIFE'S AMBITION —JERRY BRECHEISEN

TEXT: 1 THESSALONIANS 4:11,12

Make it your ambition to lead a quiet life, to mind your own business and to work with your hands, just as we told you, so that your daily life may win the respect of outsiders and so that you will not be dependent on anybody.

1. Lead a quiet life.
2. Attend to your own business.
3. Work with your hands.

WINNING AT WORK —STAN TOLER

MAIN TEXT: DANIEL 6:13

Then they said to the king, "Daniel, who is one of the exiles from Judah, pays no attention to you, O king, or to the decree you put in writing. He still prays three times a day."

1. Winners just do it!

Whatever you do, work at it with all your heart, as working for the Lord, not for men (Colossians 3:23).

    A. Our faith should impact our work.
    B. Our attitude should inspire coworkers.

2. Winners are ambassadors for God.

At this, the administrators and the satraps tried to find grounds for charges against Daniel in his conduct of government affairs, but they were unable to do so. They could find no corruption in him, because he was trustworthy and neither corrupt nor negligent. Finally these men said, "We will never find any basis for charges against this man Daniel unless it has something to do with the law of his God" (Daniel 6:4,5).

3. Winners honor God.

His work will be shown for what it is, because the Day will bring it to light. It will be revealed with fire, and the fire will test the quality of each man's work. If what he has built survives, he will receive his reward. If it is burned up, he will suffer loss; he himself will be saved, but only as one escaping through the flames (1 Corinthians 3:13-15).

QUOTES

A salesman should never be ashamed of his calling. He should be ashamed of his not calling. —Albert Lasker, quoted in *An Encyclopedia of Humor*, comp. Lowell D. Streiker (Peabody, MA: Hendrickson Publishers, 1998), n.p.

Aristotle referred to a job and leisure as "work" and that the relief from the two was called "play." —Barbara Roberts Pine, *Life with a Capital "L"* (Nashville, TN: Thomas Nelson, 1994), p. 46

Labor disgraces no man; unfortunately, you occasionally find men who disgrace labor. —Ulysses S. Grant

Without ambition, one starts nothing. Without work, one finishes nothing. The prize will not be sent to you, you have to win it. —Ralph Waldo Emerson, quoted in *Dynamic Illustrations*, ed. King Duncan (July/August/September 1999), n.p.

Life is a grindstone. But whether it grinds us down or polishes us up depends on us. —L. Thomas Holdcroft, quoted in *Inspiring Quotations*, comp. Albert M. Wells (Nashville: Thomas Nelson, 1988), n.p.

Unfulfilled desire is a good condition, for it gives meaning to life and drives us to live. —Elmer Towns

ILLUSTRATIONS

A CHEER FOR FISHING NETS

The *New York Times* reported an incident in an impoverished country. Relief workers distributed food to a long line of citizens who waited quietly in line.

But when they distributed fishing nets, the same people cheered. —King Duncan, ed., *Dynamic Illustrations* (July/August/September 1999), n.p.

TURTLE RACE CHEERLEADER

A supervisor stopped to watch a part-time worker. It was taking him forever to mop a tiny portion of the floor in a fast food restaurant.

"Have you ever been to the zoo?" she asked.

"Once when I was a little child," the worker replied. "Why?"

"Just wondering," she commented. "I can just picture you cheering for the turtle races." —King Duncan, ed., *Dynamic Illustrations* (July/August/September 1999), n.p.

THAT DAY OFF

So you want the day off. Let's take a moment to look at what you are asking for.

1. There are 365 days available for work.
2. There are 52 weeks per year, of which you already have 2 days off each weekend, leaving 261 days left available for work.
3. Since you spend 16 hours each day away from work, that accounts for 170 days. There are 91 left available for work.
4. You spend 30 minutes each day on breaks, that accounts for 23 days a year, leaving 68 days available for work.
5. You spend 1 hour a day at lunch, accounting for another 46 days per year, leaving 22 days available for work.
6. You spend 2 days per year on sick leave, leaving 20 days available for work.
7. You take 9 holidays per year, leaving 11 days available for work.
8. You take 10 vacation days each year, leaving 1 day left available for work.

No way are you going to take *that* day off. —Author unknown

SALARY RANGE?

"What salary range are we looking at?" the human resources person asked a young college graduate.

"Oh, I'd say in the neighborhood of about $80,000," he replied.

"What if I doubled that amount?" she asked.

"You must be kidding!" the astonished job applicant remarked.

She replied quickly, "You're right! But don't forget, you started it." —King Duncan, ed., *Dynamic Illustrations* (July/August/September 1999), n.p.

ILLUSTRATIONS

CAN'T YOUR FAMILY GET ALONG?

A factory worker was bragging to his coworkers, "Yes, there is a proud fighting tradition in my family! My great-great-grandfather stood his ground at Bunker Hill. Then, Great-grandfather valiantly joined up with the troops to destroy the Germans. My grandfather was at Pearl Harbor. And my father fought the North Koreans."

"Mercy!" one of the co-workers remarked. "Can't your family get along with anyone?" —Stan Toler

ANY JOB IS A BED OF ROSES

TV announcer Ed McMahon was known as one of the hardest working men in show business. He said working with his uncle in the plumbing business, he once was assigned to clean out the sewage pipes at the local Elks Club. McMahon claimed it made him realize that he could do any job on earth and be happy doing it—because any job was a bed of roses compared to cleaning out the sewage pipes. —King Duncan, ed., *Dynamic Illustrations* (July/August/September 1999), n.p.

MARTIN LUTHER KING, JR. DAY

For he himself is our peace, who has made the two one and has destroyed the barrier, the dividing wall of hostility. Ephesians 2:14

In God's eyes there has never been race, color or national origin. All people groups are equally loved and possess the same natural rights—the right to be saved by the blood of the Lord Jesus Christ. Those who are called by His name will seek to carry that truth across every cultural barrier. To them, the Great Commandment is equally important as the Great Commission.

In 1983, President Ronald Reagan signed into law a bill for the celebration of a Martin Luther King, Jr. Day. Martin Luther King, Jr. is best known for his peaceful civil rights activism. An African-American, King knew well the prejudice and social injustice committed against African-Americans in the history of our country. King peacefully organized protest marches and even encouraged African-Americans to quietly go to jail if necessary. His highly moving and beautifully written speech about his dreams for civil liberty is, perhaps, the best-known public speech on civil rights ever given (for a copy of King's "I Have a Dream" speech, see Elmer L. Towns and Stan Toler, *The Year-Round Church Event Book* [Ventura, CA: Gospel Light, 1998], pp. 54-56).

King's dreams for racial equality in America have been long in coming. But this holiday is set aside to mark the significant and costly contribution that King, and those of kindred spirit, have made to our society. Martin Luther King, Jr. Day stands out as a day to celebrate the God-given rights of every citizen on planet Earth.

SERMON
SKETCHES

SERMON SKETCH

RACE RELATIONS SUNDAY

HOW CAN I BE DELIVERED FROM MY PREJUDICED FEELINGS? —STAN TOLER

MAIN TEXT: JAMES 2:1-12

A. The age-old problem of prejudice

My brothers, as believers in our glorious Lord Jesus Christ, don't show favoritism (v. 1).

   Types of prejudice
   a. Economic
   b. Academic
   c. Sexual
   d. Racial
   e. Social

B. The difficulty of judgmental Christianity

Suppose a man comes into your meeting wearing a gold ring and fine clothes, and a poor man in shabby clothes also comes in (v. 2).

C. The power of a Christlike attitude toward all races

If you show special attention to the man wearing fine clothes and say, "Here's a good seat for you," but say to the poor man, "You stand there" or "Sit on the floor by my feet," have you not discriminated among yourselves and become judges with evil thoughts? Listen, my dear brothers: Has not God chosen those who are poor in the eyes of the world to be rich in faith and to inherit the kingdom he promised those who love him? But you have insulted the poor. Is it not the rich who are exploiting you? Are they not the ones who are dragging you into court? Are they not the ones who are slandering the noble name of him to whom you belong? If you really keep the royal law found in Scripture, "Love your neighbor as yourself," you are doing right. But if you show favoritism, you sin and are convicted by the law as lawbreakers. For whoever keeps the whole law and yet stumbles at just one point is guilty of breaking all of it. For he who said, "Do not commit adultery," also said, "Do not murder." If you do not commit adultery but do commit murder, you have become a lawbreaker (vv. 3-11).

   1. Love should be the law of life.
   2. The Golden Rule is still the only rule.

102

QUOTES

Those who claim they've never made mistakes are not honest. Those who continually make the same mistakes are not learning. —Elmer Towns

Our people have been renewed by messengers of God to face the days ahead with confidence. Martin Luther King, Jr., and other prophets, have grasped their given moments with poetic imagination and a compelling amnesia for past circumstances. —Rodger Hall Reed, Sr., quoted in the Congress of National Black Churches, Inc. (CNBC), *The African-American Devotional Bible* (Grand Rapids, MI: Zondervan Publishing House, 1997), p. 40.

If any of you are around when I have to meet my day, I don't want a long speech. I'd like somebody to mention that day that Martin Luther King, Jr. tried to love somebody. I want you to say that day that I tried to be like and to walk with them. —Martin Luther King, Jr.

God hasten the time when every minister will become a registered voter and a part of every movement for the betterment of our people. —Martin Luther King, Jr.

GIVE AN ACCOUNT OF OUR DREAMS

If Dr. King were alive today, he would ask us to give an account of our dreams, not his. He would ask us, "What have you done in my absence? Did I die for nothing? Have you moved toward freedom and justice for all? Are you finally at peace or are you still fighting pointless wars?" —Marjorie L. Kimbrough, quoted in *The Abingdon Preaching Annual 1996*, ed. Michael Duduit (Nashville, TN: Abingdon Press, 1995), n.p.

Charles Willie, a classmate of Dr. King, writes, "By exalting the accomplishments of Martin Luther King, Jr., we fail to recognize his humanity—his personal and public struggles—which are similar to yours and mine. By idolizing those whom we honor, we fail to realize that we could go and do likewise." —David J. Garrow, *Bearing the Cross: Martin Luther King, Jr., and the Southern Christian Leadership Conference* (New York: Vintage, 1998), p. 23.

DEALING WITH DRAGONS

We can't be responsible for the irreconcilable, mean, and nasty people in our lives—even the ones related to us—but we are completely responsible for how we react to them. In a world of dragons—even when those dragons are members of the family—our Lord has not given us permission to breathe fire. —Robert R. Kopp, "Mother's Day/Father's Day," *The Abingdon Preaching Annual 1996*, ed. Michael Duduit (Nashville, TN: Abingdon Press, 1995).

103

ILLUSTRATIONS

ILLUSTRATIONS

MARTIN LUTHER KING JR.'S BIOGRAPHY

Born in Atlanta on January 15, 1929, Martin Luther King, Jr.'s roots were in the African-American Baptist church. He was the grandson of the Rev. A. D. Williams, pastor of Ebenezer Baptist Church and a founder of Atlanta's NAACP chapter, and the son of Martin Luther King, Sr., who succeeded Williams as Ebenezer's pastor and also became a civil rights leader. He greatly admired black social gospel proponents who saw the Church as an instrument for improving the lives of African-Americans. Graduating from Moorehouse College, he continued theological studies at Crozer Theological Seminary in Chester, Pennsylvania, and at Boston University, where he received a doctorate in systematic theology in 1955. Rejecting offers for academic positions, King decided while completing his Ph. D. requirements to return to the South and accept the pastorate of Dexter Avenue Baptist Church in Montgomery, Alabama. —Clayborne Carson, *King's Biography.*

http://stanford/edu/group/King/Biography/briefbio.html (accessed October, 4, 1999).

MOTHER'S DAY

—

When Jesus saw his mother there, and the disciple whom he loved standing nearby, he said to his mother, "Dear woman, here is your son," and to the disciple, "Here is your mother." From that time on, this disciple took her into his home. John 19:26,27

Jesus' honoring of His mother not only came from His love and devotion to her, but also from His obedience to God's law. Our honoring of mothers and fathers strengthens the institution of the home and acknowledges the rule of God's law in our lives.

While Mother's Day was officially proclaimed in the United States in 1914, celebrations honoring mothers was not a new idea. The ancient Greeks held their own honorary celebrations, and in seventeenth century England, a special "Mothering Sunday" was observed.[1] The celebration of motherhood is an ageless tradition. Our sense of gratefulness and attachment is inherent within our very natures.

Mother's Day in the United States was organized for slightly different reasons than we celebrate it today. In 1872, Julia Ward Howe suggested it as a day dedicated to peace.[2] Anna Jarvis resumed the organization of the day in 1907 as a day called "Mother's Friendship Day." This was intended to be a day to heal the scars of the Civil War.[3] A special day to honor mothers caught on quickly in the United States, and on May 8, 1914, Congress designated the second Sunday in May as Mother's Day. From that point in time, Mother's Day quickly grew to become a sentimental national holiday.

SERMON
SKETCHES

SERMON SKETCH

WHAT HAPPENS WHEN MOTHERS PRAY? —STAN TOLER

MAIN TEXT: 1 SAMUEL 1:1-28

   A. Hannah was a model of motherhood.
      1.   She was a loving wife.

But to Hannah he gave a double portion because he loved her, and the LORD had closed her womb (v. 5).

      2.   She was a church-going wife.

This went on year after year. Whenever Hannah went up to the house of the LORD, her rival provoked her till she wept and would not eat (v. 7).

      3.   She was desiring to be a mother.

Hannah was praying in her heart, and her lips were moving but her voice was not heard. Eli thought she was drunk and said to her, "How long will you keep on getting drunk? Get rid of your wine." "Not so, my Lord," Hannah replied, "I am a woman who is deeply troubled. I have not been drinking wine or beer; I was pouring out my soul to the LORD. Do not take your servant for a wicked woman; I have been praying here out of my great anguish and grief" (vv. 13-16).

      4.   She was a godly wife.

Each year his mother made him a little robe and took it to him when she went up with her husband to offer the annual sacrifice (1 Samuel 2:19).

   B. Hannah was an overcomer of problems.
      1.   She wanted a child, but she was barren.

He had two wives; one was called Hannah and the other Peninnah. Peninnah had children, but Hannah had none (v. 2).

      2.   She was a sensitive soul.

And because the LORD had closed her womb, her rival kept provoking her in order to irritate her. This went on year after year. Whenever Hannah went up to the house of the LORD, her rival provoked her till she wept and would not eat (vv. 6,7).

3. She had an obvious problem.

In bitterness of soul Hannah wept much and prayed to the LORD (v. 10).

C. Hannah was a prayer warrior.
  1. She committed her child to God.

And she made a vow, saying, "O LORD Almighty, if you will only look upon your servant's misery and remember me, and not forget your servant but give her a son, then I will give him to the LORD for all the days of his life, and no razor will ever be used on his head" (v. 11).

  2. She never ceased praying for a child.

As she kept on praying to the LORD, Eli observed her mouth (v. 12).

  3. She believed God would answer.

She said, "May your servant find favor in your eyes." Then she went her way and ate something, and her face was no longer downcast. Early the next morning they arose and worshiped before the LORD and then went back to their home at Ramah. Elkanah lay with Hannah his wife, and the LORD remembered her (vv. 18,19).

D. Hannah's prayer brought results.
  1. God gave her a son.

And the boy Samuel continued to grow in stature and in favor with the LORD and with men (1 Samuel 2:26).

  2. Her son went into the ministry.

The LORD called Samuel a third time, and Samuel got up and went to Eli and said, "Here I am; you called me." Then Eli realized that the LORD was calling the boy (1 Samuel 3:8).

  3. Her son followed her example in prayer.

The people all said to Samuel, "Pray to the LORD your God for your servants so that we will not die, for we have added to all our other sins the evil of asking for a king" (1 Samuel 12:19).

SERMON
SKETCHES

ESTHER —JERRY BRECHEISEN

MAIN TEXT: ESTHER 2:5-17

1. Her Call (v. 8)

When the king's order and edict had been proclaimed, many girls were brought to the citadel of Susa and put under the care of Hegai. Esther also was taken to the king's palace and entrusted to Hegai, who had charge of the harem.

2. Her Character (v. 9)

The girl pleased him and won his favor. Immediately he provided her with her beauty treatments and special food. He assigned to her seven maids selected from the king's palace and moved her and her maids into the best place in the harem.

3. Her Coronation (v. 17)

Now the king was attracted to Esther more than to any of the other women, and she won his favor and approval more than any of the other virgins. So he set a royal crown on her head and made her queen instead of Vashti.

THE DYNAMICS BEHIND A DANIEL —ELMER TOWNS

MAIN TEXT: DANIEL 1:1-15

1. Somebody taught.

The king assigned them a daily amount of food and wine from the king's table. They were to be trained for three years, and after that they were to enter the king's service. Among these were some from Judah: Daniel, Hananiah, Mishael and Azariah. The chief official gave them new names: to Daniel, the name Belteshazzar; to Hananiah, Shadrach; to Mishael, Meshach; and to Azariah, Abednego. But Daniel resolved not to defile himself with the royal food and wine, and he asked the chief official for permission not to defile himself this way (vv. 5-8).

2. Somebody listened.

Now God had caused the official to show favor and sympathy to Daniel, but the official told Daniel, "I am afraid of my Lord the king, who has assigned your food and drink. Why should he see you looking worse than the other young men your age? The king would then have my head because of you." Daniel then said to the guard whom the chief official had appointed over Daniel, Hananiah, Mishael and Azariah, "Please test your servants for ten days: Give us nothing but vegetables to eat and water to drink. Then compare our appearance with that of the young men who eat the royal food, and treat your servants in accordance with what you see." So he agreed to this and tested them for ten days. At the end of the ten days they looked healthier and better nourished than any of the young men who ate the royal food (vv. 9-15).

SERMON SKETCHES

HOW A MOTHER PRAYED —ELMER TOWNS

MAIN TEXT: 1 SAMUEL 1:1-20

1. Decisively

   And she made a vow, saying, "O LORD Almighty, if you will only look upon your servant's misery and remember me, and not forget your servant but give her a son (v. 11).

2. Specifically

   Then I will give him to the LORD for all the days of his life, and no razor will ever be used on his head (v. 11).

3. Continually

   Hannah was praying in her heart, and her lips were moving but her voice was not heard. Eli thought she was drunk (v. 13).

4. Persistently

   As she kept on praying to the LORD, Eli observed her mouth (v. 12).

5. Obediently

   Not so, my Lord," Hannah replied, "I am a woman who is deeply troubled. I have not been drinking wine or beer; I was pouring out my soul to the LORD (v. 15).

6. Expectantly

   She said, "May your servant find favor in your eyes." Then she went her way and ate something, and her face was no longer downcast (v. 18).

QUOTES

The mother-in-law remembers not that she was a daughter-in-law. —A proverb

Motherhood is full of frustrations and challenges—but eventually they move out. —Angela Akers and King Duncan, eds., *Amusing Grace* (Knoxville, TN: Seven Worlds Corporation, 1993), n.p.

Mother made me believe that the average person can rise above circumstances even with limited resources and in difficult circumstances, and get the job done. —Elmer Towns

Franklin Roosevelt reported that even after he became president of the United States, he never went outdoors without his mother calling after him, "Franklin! Are you sure you're dressed warmly enough?" —Angela Akers and King Duncan, eds., *Amusing Grace* (Knoxville, TN: Seven Worlds Corporation, 1993), n.p.

MY SUNSET PRAYER

As once she stroked my tiny head
With a softness like the sand,
I touch her thin and silv'ry strands
And hold her trembling hand;
As once she viewed my learning feet
With a firm but anxious care,
I watch her failing, bending gait
And breathe my sunset prayer,
"O LORD, since I'm her precious child
From some great other time,
Help me to love her even more,
Since the years have made her mine." —Jerry Brecheisen

My mother was the one who made me work, made me believe that one day it would be possible for me to walk without braces. —Wilma Rudolph

Mothers fill places so great that there isn't an angel in heaven who wouldn't be glad to give a bushel of diamonds to come down here and take their place. —Billy Sunday, quoted in *Inspiring Quotations*, ed. Albert Wells, Jr. (Nashville, TN: Thomas Nelson, 1988), p. 14.

Mothers exercise the greatest influences on our self-perception because we are the extension of their dreams, values and prejudices. A mother usually expects her children to become more than she became and accomplish more than she achieved. —Elmer Towns

Children brighten the home. Which one of them ever turns off a light? —Christian Herald

A MOTHER'S LOVE DETERMINES HOW

A mother's love determines how
We love ourselves and others.
There is no sky we'll ever see
Not lit by that first love.

Stripped of love, the universe
Would drive us mad with pain;
But we are born into a world
That greets our cries with joy.

How much I owe you for the kiss
That told me who I was!
The greatest gift—a love of life—
Lay laughing in your eyes.

Because of you my world still has
The soft grace of your smile;
And every wind of fortune bears
The scent of your caress. —Nicholas Gordon, *Poetry by Nicholas Gordon.* http://www.members.aol.com/nickgo (accessed October 9, 1999).

Who else but a mother can show joy over receiving a sixty-four ounce bottle of perfume with a dollar and twenty-five cent price tag on it? —Lowell D. Streiker, comp., *An Encyclopedia of Humor* (Peabody, MA: Hendrickson Publishers, 1998), p. 82.

We can do no great things—only small things with great love. —Mother Teresa

There's only one child in the world, and every mother has it. —English proverb

The day the child realizes that all adults are imperfect, he becomes an adolescent. The day he forgives them, he becomes an adult. The day he forgives himself, he becomes wise. —Robert R. Kopp, "Mother's Day/Father's Day," Michael Duduit, ed., *The Abingdon Preaching Annual 1996* (Nashville, TN: Abingdon Press, 1995), p. 19.

Simply having children does not make mothers. —A. Shedd, "Salt from My Attic" in *Encyclopedia of 7700 Illustrations*, Paul Lee Tan (Rockville, MD: Assurance Publishers, 1979), p. 863.

ILLUSTRATIONS

ILLUSTRATIONS

SAY WHAT MOM SAYS

On a steaming hot day, family guests were seated around the table. Mother asked her four-year-old to say grace.

"I don't know what to say!" the little boy responded.

"Just say what you've heard your Mom say," the mother replied.

The little boy bowed reverently, "Lord! Why did I invite these folks on a day like this?!" —Author unknown

THE GRANDMOTHER OF US ALL

Henrietta Mears has been called the "Mother of Sunday School." But I like to think of her more as the "grandmother" of modern evangelicalism. She used to say, "There is no magic in small plans. When I consider my ministry, I think of the world. Anything less than that would not be worthy of Christ nor of his will for my life." So while inspiring her "college boys" with her hats, she also imparted to them the vision of conquering the world for Christ. And her "boys" included the likes of Campus Crusade's Bill Bright and former U.S. Senate chaplain, the late Richard Halverson. —Wendy Murray Zoba, "The Grandmother of Us All," *Christianity Today* (September 16, 1996). http://www.christianity.net/ct/6TA/6TA044.html (accessed October 4, 1999).

MOTHERS' PRAYERS CHANGING THE DIRECTION OF THE WORLD

Every Monday morning, newspapers splash the grisly reports of new killings from across Brazil. Maria Santos breathes a prayer of thanks that her son, Roberto's name is not among the weekend's dead.

. . . Nearly 600 children are murdered annually in Rio de Janeiro alone. . . . Even for Christian kids, sexual immorality, occult spiritism, depression, drug use and materialism threaten to unravel their commitment to Christ.

At one time, Santos focused her prayers solely on her son. But now she prays alongside 15,000 mothers in the growing movement "Wake Up, Deborah," which is rallying the church to the spiritual potential within Brazilian youth. The group's name is inspired from the uncertain and troubling period in Israel's history noted in Judges 4 and 5 when the prophetess Deborah woke up the Israelites against the oppressors.

. . . "Wake Up, Deborah" members pledge to pray at least 15 minutes a day that their children will become not only Christians, but missionaries—to their communities, to Brazil, and to the world.

"Women don't have a second-hand calling," [director Ana Maria] Pereira says. "Multitudes are walking toward hell. Our prayers can change the direction of the world." —Debra Fleetwood Wood, "Mothers Movement Awakens Missions," *Christianity Today* (May 19, 1997). http://www.christianity.net/ct/7T6/7T6045.html (accessed October 4, 1999).

MAMA TOLD ME NOT TO

I always remember a comment by Judge Elbert Tuttle, one of the great jurists of our country. A Republican appointed by President Eisenhower, he made some of the most definitive and courageous rulings on civil rights during the troubled segregation days in Georgia. Walter Cronkite once interviewed him. "Judge Tuttle, I understand you've never drunk whiskey."

The judge said, "I've never in my life tasted an alcoholic drink."

Cronkite asked, "Why not?"

The judge gave a simple reply, "Because my mama told me not to." —Jimmy Carter, *Living Faith* (New York: Random House, 1996), p. 58.

GRANT'S MOTHER

When General Grant's mother died, he said to the minister who was to officiate at the funeral: "Make no reference to me. She owed nothing to me. Speak of her just as she was, a pure-minded, simple-hearted, earnest Christian." —Clarence Macartney, *Macartney's Illustrations* (New York: Abingdon Press, 1955), n.p.

ERIN'S PRIDE

When I was 13, I built a pigeon coop and raced pigeons with the local Racing Pigeon Association. Pigeon owners don't let the birds eat wet corn, since the grain will swell up in their gullets and choke them.

One night some grain that I had left for the pigeons became wet overnight. My prize pigeon ate it and her gullet swelled.

"She's gonna die," I yelled, and ran into the house to tell Mother. After several procedures failed, she announced, "We'll operate."

"She'll die," I said.

"She'll die anyway," Mother replied.

The dining room table became the operating table. Mother sterilized the "equipment," plucked the feathers from the pigeon's neck, and washed it with alcohol.

With a single incision, she sliced the bird's neck from the head to breast. The bird flayed, but I held the wings steady. Mother thrust her fingers into its neck and retrieved the corn. Then, using a sterilized needle and sewing thread, she stitched the bird's neck back together. "Just like darning a sock," she said.

The pigeon lived and I called her "Erin's Pride," after my mother. Later, Erin's Pride won the 500-mile race from Gulf Port, Mississippi, to Savannah, Georgia.

"We're Townses," she had previously announced. " We can do anything we want to do." —Elmer Towns

ILLUSTRATIONS

115

REFRIGERATOR ARTWORK

A man spent a great sum of money on a brand new computer. It had the latest in word processing and desktop publishing capabilities.

Wanting to impress his mother, he wrote her a long letter in a beautiful typeface and illustrated it with elaborate clip art. Several days later, he called to see if she received the letter.

"Yes, I received it. Son, you did a fine job. I hung it by your other picture on the refrigerator." —Angela Akers and King Duncan, eds., *Amusing Grace* (Knoxville, TN: Seven Worlds Corporation, 1993), n.p.

MOTHER'S TEN COMMANDMENTS OF EATING

1. Of all the beasts of the field, and of the fish of the sea shalt thou eat. But of the leaves of the tree, thou shalt not eat thereof. For in the day that thou eatest, thou shalt surely get a stomachache.
2. Thou shalt drink of all the good liquids I have given unto thee. Only let not thy liquids be spilled onto thy clothing nor onto thy neighbor's clothing.
3. When thou sittest in thy chair, thou shalt not place thy feet on the table nor over thine head. For that is an abomination to me.
4. Thou shalt not pour Kool-Aid over thy mashed potatoes, nor use it as a dip for thy celery, nor spill it over the floor of the place of eating.
5. When thou hast drunk of thy cup, it shall not be held to thy face as a mask, nor used to strike thy brother or thy sister upon their head.
6. Thou shalt not eat thy macaroni with thine hands. Neither shalt thou distribute it widely over the place where thou livest.
7. Thy brussel sprouts shalt not be made into any graven image in the place where thou eatest. That is an abomination to me.
8. When thou sittest in thine chair, thou shalt not slideth down therein.
9. Remember thy mealtime to arrive when I calleth thee. Three meals thou hast been given to cause thy borders to increase.
10. If thou keepest all these commandments I have given unto thee, thou shalt be perfect in my sight, and perfect in my neighbor's sight. —Jerry Brecheisen

I DIDN'T DO ANYTHING TODAY

One day, a father came home from work to find his home in total chaos. The children were playing on the lawn in their pajamas. The front door was open. Inside, the furniture was scattered. A shattered lamp lay on the floor. The TV was blaring.

In the kitchen, the sink was full of stacked dishes and cereal was spilled on the floor. Heading upstairs to the bedroom, he passed clothing strung along the banister, stepped over toys on the steps, and climbed over a plant that had spilled onto the floor.

In the bedroom, he was shocked to see his wife still in bed, watching a talk show on the spare TV. She asked how his day went.

He replied, "What in the world has happened here?!"

She answered, "Well, every day, when you arrive home from work, you ask me if I did anything today."

"And?"

"And today I didn't!" —Author unknown. http://www.gcfl.net (no access date).

A CONCERNED MOTHER

One wintry morning, a concerned mother called the school principal. She wanted to know if her son's bus had arrived yet. When asked what grade he was in, the mother replied,

"Oh, he is not one of the students, he drives the bus!" —Angela Akers and King Duncan, eds., *Amusing Grace* (Knoxville, TN: Seven Worlds Corporation, 1993), n.p.

BEDTIME PRAYERS

A mother was hearing her little girl's bedtime prayers. The little girl asked, "Is Grandma still downstairs?"

"Yes, she is," her mother replied.

The little girl continued her prayer, but raised the volume to a yell, "And God, you know how much I want a computer . . ."

Mother interrupted, "You don't have to yell, honey, God's not deaf."

The little girl replied, "I know, but Grandma is." —Michael P. Green, ed., *Illustrations for Biblical Preaching* (Grand Rapids, MI: Baker Book House, 1996), n.p.

ILLUSTRATIONS

BABY COMFORTS MOTHER

A young mother had a totally exasperating day. The two-year-old had written with a crayon all over the living room wall. The washing machine broke. The VCR quit working. And the dog chewed through the kitchen wall telephone wire.

Totally frustrated, the mom sat on a chair beside her one-year-old, who was splashing in the bowl of Jell-O on her high-chair tray. Soon the frustrated mom put her arm on the tray, buried her head in her arm and began to sob.

With a sticky hand and a warm heart, the one-year-old took her pacifier out of her mouth and pushed it into her mother's mouth. And with the other sticky hand, she calmly patted her mother on the head. —Author unknown

WHEN I FALL DOWN

On a Mother's Day card: "Now that we have a mature, adult relationship, there is something I'd like to tell you. You're still the first person I think of when I fall down and go boom!" —Derl G. Keefer

THE PRINCESS AND THE FROG

Once upon a time a beautiful princess encountered a frog in a pond.

The frog spoke to the princess: "I used to be a handsome prince until someone put an evil spell on me. If you kiss me on my nose, I will become a prince once again. Then we can be married and move into my mother's castle; and you can clean the castle, bear children, cook the meals and live happily ever after with your handsome prince."

The beautiful princess had frog legs for supper. —Elmer Towns

THE BIGGEST PIECE

Sitting around the family table for supper, the youngest child spotted the dessert. With eager hands he reached for the biggest piece of chocolate cake on the plate.

Grabbing his hand with a scolding look, the mother said, "Son, I'm ashamed of you! Why did you take the biggest piece?"

The son replied with chocolate frosting all over his face, "Well, Mom, with this bunch, it looked to me like that was the only way I was gonna get it!" —Author unknown

118

A NORMAL FAMILY

It's getting more difficult to define a "normal family." In one stepparent home, the sister went to her real father's home every other weekend. The brother stayed with his mother and father. As she was leaving the house, he commented, "Must be nice to get a new family every other weekend. I'm stuck here with the same one!" —Adapted from *Annie's Homepage.* http://www.annieshomepage.com/motherday.html (no access date).

YOUR WIFE AND I HAVEN'T BEEN GETTING ALONG

Father came home from work and found his young daughter sitting under a tree by the driveway. Noticing her sad countenance, he inquired, "What's wrong, dear?"

She replied, "Well, Dad, your wife and I haven't been getting along that great today." —William Turner, quoted in *The Abingdon Preaching Annual 1998*, ed. Michael Duduit (Nashville, TN: Abingdon Press, 1997), n.p.

WORST CASE SCENARIO

In the cartoon, *Calvin and Hobbes*, Calvin asks his mother:
"Can Hobbes and I go play in the rain?"
Mom replies, "Of course not!"
"Why?" Calvin asks.
"You'll get soaked."
Calvin replies, "What's wrong with getting soaked?"
Mom answers, "You could catch cold, run up a big doctor bill, linger for a few months and then die."
Calvin looks forlornly out the window. "I forgot. If you ask a mom, you always get a worse-case scenario." —Bill Watterson, *The Essential Calvin and Hobbes*®, quoted in Angela Akers and King Duncan, ed., *Amusing Grace* (Knoxville, TN: Seven Worlds Corporation, 1993).

THE CHANGING SERMON

When a young minister was still single, he preached a sermon entitled "Rules for Raising Children." After he got married and had children of his own, he changed the title of the sermon to "Suggestions for Raising Children." When his children got to be teenagers, he stopped preaching on that subject altogether. —Rev. Bernard Brunsting

NATIONAL DAY OF PRAYER

I urge, then, first of all, that requests, prayers, intercession and thanksgiving be made for everyone—for kings and all those in authority, that we may live peaceful and quiet lives in all godliness and holiness. 1 Timothy 2:1,2

There is a sense of urgency in Paul's request—a sense that the prayers of God's people are the cornerstones of society. When they pray, peace has a chance. When they fail to pray, turmoil is inevitable.

Prayer has long been a foundation of American history. The 1776 Continental Congress of colonial America declared the very first National Day of Prayer.[1] At this time, the colonies were in a bitter struggle with Great Britain, and delegates from the thirteen colonies gathered together to pray and to try to foster reconciliation between the states and the motherland.

Various days of prayer were declared occasionally by United States presidents, but no formal measures were taken to enact it until 1952. On April 17, 1952, President Truman signed a bill requiring the United States President to select a day for national prayer each year. From this point on, presidents selected days, but it was not until 1988 that the National Day of Prayer became a fixed event on the calendar. The bill to fix this date received broad bipartisan support and became public law.[2]

Today people of various faiths participate in observing the National Day of Prayer. It is observed on the first Thursday of May, and participants are encouraged to specifically pray for their government and community leaders.

SERMON
SKETCHES

SERMON SKETCH

HOW TO MAKE THE MOST OF YOUR PRAYER LIFE —STAN TOLER

MAIN TEXT: LUKE 5:16

But Jesus often withdrew to lonely places and prayed.

There are four essential steps in making the most of your prayer life.
1. Set a specific time.
    a. Put it into your schedule; make an appointment with God.

   In the morning, O LORD, you hear my voice; in the morning I lay my requests before you and wait in expectation (Psalm 5:3).

    b. Be disciplined and prayerful.
2. Decide on a specific place.
    a. Find a "secret closet."
3. Pray with a specific purpose.
    a. Start a prayer journal.
    b. Update your prayer list.
    c. Track your answers to prayer.

SERMON
SKETCHES

HOW JESUS PRAYED —ELMER TOWNS

1.   He prayed early.

Very early in the morning, while it was still dark, Jesus got up, left the house and went off to a solitary place, where he prayed. Simon and his companions went to look for him, and when they found him, they exclaimed: "Everyone is looking for you!" (Mark 1:35-37).

2.   He prayed late.

After he had dismissed them, he went up on a mountainside by himself to pray. When evening came, he was there alone (Matthew 14:23).

3.   He prayed all night.

One of those days Jesus went out to a mountainside to pray, and spent the night praying to God (Luke 6:12).

4.   He prayed before events.

One of those days Jesus went out to a mountainside to pray, and spent the night praying to God. When morning came, he called his disciples to him and chose twelve of them, whom he also designated apostles (Luke 6:12,13).

5.   He prayed for His friends.

Simon, Simon, Satan has asked to sift you as wheat. But I have prayed for you, Simon, that your faith may not fail (Luke 22:31,32).

6.   He prayed until the heavens opened.

When all the people were being baptized, Jesus was baptized too. And as he was praying, heaven was opened (Luke 3:21).

7.   He prayed as He died.

Jesus called out with a loud voice, "Father, into your hands I commit my spirit." When he had said this, he breathed his last (Luke 23:46).

QUOTES

QUOTES

No matter where you stand on the prayer-in-school issue, one truth cannot be denied: Children will pray as long as they have math tests. —Author unknown

Prayer does not equip us for greater works—prayer is the greater work. —Oswald Chambers

History fails to record a single precedent in which nations subject to moral decay have not passed into political and economic decline. There has been either a spiritual awakening to overcome the moral lapse, or a progressive deterioration leading to ultimate national disaster. —Douglas MacArthur, quoted in *America's God and Country Encyclopedia of Quotations*, comp. William J. Federer (Coppell, TX: Fame Publishing, 1996), n.p.

STATUE OF LIBERTY INAUGURATION INVOCATION

We pray for all the nations of the earth; that in equity and charity their sure foundations may be established; that in piety and wisdom they may find a true welfare, in obedience to Thee, glory and praise; and that, in all the enlargements of their power, they may be ever the joyful servants of Him to whose holy dominion and kingdom shall be no end. —Rev. Richard S. Storrs, quoted in *America's God and Country Encyclopedia of Quotations*, comp. William J. Federer (Coppell, TX: Fame Publishing, 1996), n.p.

ILLUSTRATIONS

FORGIVE YOUR BROTHER

Johnny was upset with his brother, Willy. Before he said his prayers, Johnny's mother said to him, "Now I want you to forgive your brother." But Johnny was not in a very forgiving frame of mind. "No, I won't forgive him," he replied.

   In desperation she said, "What if your brother were to die tonight? How would you feel if you knew you hadn't forgiven him?" Johnny reluctantly conceded, "All right, I forgive him, but if he's alive in the morning, I'll get him!" —G. Stuart Briscoe, *The Family Book of Christian Values* (Colorado Springs, CO: Chariot Victor Books, 1995), p. 62

NATIONAL DAY OF PRAYER IDEAS

1. Decorate your home with red, white and blue streamers, balloons and American flags during National Day of Prayer week.
2. Have a family devotional time to talk about stories from the Bible where prayer changed people's lives.
3. Create a prayer calendar with your children.
4. Make Scripture place mats to use during the week leading up to the National Day of Prayer (NDP).
5. Organize a picnic outing around your community's NDP observance.
6. Visit a nursing home with your family. Spend time praying with the residents and interceding for our nation and its leaders.
7. Teach older children the names of their elected officials and the offices they hold.
8. Organize a bike parade up and down your street. After the parade, invite all participants into your backyard for prayers and ice cream. —Adapted from the *1995 National Day of Prayer Resource Kit.* http://www.wcg.org/wn/96feb13/prayidea.htm (no access date).

NEW YEAR'S DAY

Therefore, if anyone is in Christ, he is a new creation; the old has gone, the new has come! 2 Corinthians 5:17

The Church of the Lord Jesus Christ can celebrate newness unlike any other institution. It has experienced newness in the redemption of Christ, who made possible the change from the old life to the new. It's no wonder that Christians are comfortable celebrating the hope and new beginnings of the New Year's Day observance.

New Year's Day is a popular holiday that is celebrated around the world. People of different countries and different religious beliefs celebrate the New Year according to their own calendars. For example, Muslims celebrate the New Year based on the movements of the moon. Hindus, on the other hand, celebrate New Year at different times of the year, depending upon where they live. Similarly, people in the Far East celebrate the New Year depending on their national customs.[1]

In the United States, New Year's Day observances are usually preceded by parties and gatherings the night before, and it is often celebrated with food and football games the next day. Many people make New Year's resolutions as a means to change old habits. For the Christian, there are no widespread customs of a spiritual nature. However, some churches traditionally find New Year's to be an appropriate time to encourage Christians to make spiritual resolutions for the upcoming year. Some churches hold candlelight vigils on New Year's Eve to welcome in the new year with prayer and dedication to God.

SERMON SKETCH

STARTING OVER —ELMER TOWNS

MAIN TEXT: HAGGAI 2:15-18

"Now give careful thought to this from this day on—consider how things were before one stone was laid on another in the LORD's temple. When anyone came to a heap of twenty measures, there were only ten. When anyone went to a wine vat to draw fifty measures, there were only twenty. I struck all the work of your hands with blight, mildew and hail, yet you did not turn to me," declares the LORD. "From this day on, from this twenty-fourth day of the ninth month, give careful thought to the day when the foundation of the LORD's temple was laid. Give careful thought."

Know why you failed.
1. Know your motives
   a. Some mistakes come from sin (intentional).
   b. Some mistakes are not your fault (unintentional).
2. Know your circumstances and examine why you failed and change the process.
3. Know your enemy (see 1 Peter 5:8).
4. Know your weaknesses.
5. Determine to learn from the mistakes of others.

SERMON
SKETCHES

A VISION FOR THE FUTURE —STAN TOLER

MAIN TEXT: ACTS 26:19

So then, King Agrippa, I was not disobedient to the vision from heaven.

1.   What is a vision?

Where there is no revelation, the people cast off restraint; but blessed is he who keeps the law (Proverbs 29:18).

A vision is a clear picture and an accurate understanding of God, yourself, and your circumstances. —George Barna

2.   What hinders the vision?

On one of these journeys I was going to Damascus with the authority and commission of the chief priests. About noon, O king, as I was on the road, I saw a light from heaven, brighter than the sun, blazing around me and my companions. We all fell to the ground, and I heard a voice saying to me in Aramaic, "Saul, Saul, why do you persecute me? It is hard for you to kick against the goads." Then I asked, "Who are you, Lord?" "I am Jesus, whom you are persecuting," the Lord replied. "Now get up and stand on your feet. I have appeared to you to appoint you as a servant and as a witness of what you have seen of me and what I will show you" (Acts 26:12-16).

   A. Bad Attitudes
   B. A Critical Spirit
   C. Internal Conflict
   D. Sinful Unbelief

3.   What defines the vision?

So then, King Agrippa, I was not disobedient to the vision from heaven. First to those in Damascus, then to those in Jerusalem and in all Judea, and to the Gentiles also, I preached that they should repent and turn to God and prove their repentance by their deeds (Acts 26:19,20).

   A. Who are we?
   B. What's our address?
   C. What time is it?
   D. Whose church is this?

128

QUOTES

A.D. The world writes these letters carelessly as it turns the page to record for the first time the new year; but in these letters is the open secret of the ages, this too, is a year of our Lord, and an acceptable year, a year of grace. —Jesse B. Thomas, quoted in *Five Thousand Best Modern Illustrations*, ed. G.B.F. Hallock (New York: R. R. Smith, 1931), n.p.

People laugh at New Year's resolutions. But we all can use ten minutes in a chair followed by a humble prayer. —Albert Wells, Jr., ed., *Inspiring Quotations* (Nashville, TN: Thomas Nelson, 1988), n.p.

I ASKED THE NEW YEAR

I asked the New Year for some message sweet,
Some rule of life with which to guide my feet;
I asked, and paused; he answered soft and low,
God's will to know!
"Will knowledge then suffice, New Year?" I cried;
And ere the question into silence died,
The answer came, "Nay, but remember, too, God's will to do!"
Once more I asked, "Is there no more to tell?"
And once again the answer sweetly fell,
"Yes! This thing, all other things above: God's will to love!" —Albert Wells,
 Jr., ed., *Inspiring Quotations* (Nashville, TN: Thomas Nelson, 1988), n.p.

Good resolutions are like babies crying in church. They should be carried out immediately. —Charles M. Sheldon, quoted in *Inspiring Quotations*, ed. Albert Wells, Jr. (Nashville, TN: Thomas Nelson, 1988), n.p.

GOD BLESS YOUR YEAR

God bless your year!
Your coming in, your going out,
Your rest, your traveling about,
The tough, the smooth,
The bright, the drear',
God bless your year! —Albert Wells, Jr., ed., *Inspiring Quotations* (Nashville, TN: Thomas Nelson, 1988), n.p.

129

QUOTES

LET ME DEDICATE ALL THIS YEAR TO THEE

Father, let me dedicate
All this year to Thee,
In whatever worldly state
Thou wilt have me be:
Not from sorrow, pain, or care,
Freedom dare I claim;
This alone shall be my prayer:
Glorify Thy name.

Can a child presume to choose
Where or how to live?
Can a Father's love refuse
All the best to give?
More Thou givest every day
Than the best can claim,
Nor withholdest aught that may
Glorify Thy name.

If on life, serene and fair,
Brighter rays may shine;
If in mercy Thou wilt spare
Joys that yet are mine;
Let my glad heart, while it sings,
Thee in all proclaim,
And what'er the future brings,
Glorify Thy name. —Lawrence Tuttiett, quoted in *Inspiring
Quotations*, ed. Albert Wells, Jr. (Nashville, TN: Thomas
Nelson, 1988), n.p.

Be at war with your vices, at peace with your neighbors, and let every new
year find you a better man. —Benjamin Franklin, quoted in *Inspiring
Quotations*, ed. Albert Wells, Jr. (Nashville, TN: Thomas Nelson, 1988), n.p.

AULD LANG SYNE

Should auld acquaintance be forgot,
And never brought to mind?
Should auld acquaintance be forgot,
And the days of auld lang syne! —Robert Burns (1759-1796)

NEW YEAR'S

The wave is breaking on the shore—
The echo fading from the chime—
Again the shadow moveth o'er
The dial-plate of time! —John Greenleaf Whittier, quoted in
Five Thousand Best Modern Illustrations, ed. G.B.F. Hallock
(New York: R. R. Smith, 1931), p. 527.

MISTAKES

Mistakes are friends that help me see myself.
Mistakes are keys that unlock the door of opportunity.
Mistakes are windows that help me look at the world.
Mistakes are prophecies that help me understand the
future.
Mistakes are teachers that give me insight into life.
Mistakes are poetry that help me see how things fit
together.
Mistakes are the paint I use for the portrait of life.
—Elmer Towns

INTO THE COMING YEAR

With every power for good to stay and guide me,
Comforted and inspired beyond all fear,
I'll live these days with [God]
In thought beside me,
And pass with You into
Into the coming year. —Dietrich Bonhoeffer, quoted in
Inspiring Quotations, ed. Albert Wells, Jr. (Nashville, TN:
Thomas Nelson, 1988), n.p.

QUOTES

I WILL START ANEW THIS MORNING

I will start anew this morning
With a higher, fairer creed;
I will cease to stand complaining
Of my ruthless neighbor's greed;
I will cease to sit repining
While my duty's call is clear;
I will waste no moment whining,
And my heart shall know no fear.

I will not be swayed by envy
When my rival's strength is shown;
I will not deny his merit,
But I'll strive to prove my own:
I will try to see the beauty
Spread before me, rain or shine;
I will cease to preach Your duty,
And be more concerned with mine. —Bonnie Yarnell,
quoted in *Inspiring Quotations*, ed. Albert Wells, Jr. (Nashville,
TN: Thomas Nelson, 1988), n.p.

I said to the man who stands at the Gate of the Year, "Give me light that I
may tread softly into the unknown!"

And he replied, "Step into the darkness, put your hand into the hand
of God, and that will be to you better than a light and safer than a known
way!" —King George VI, quoted in *Inspiring Quotations*, ed. Albert Wells, Jr.
(Nashville, TN: Thomas Nelson, 1988), n.p.

You can never change the past. But by the grace of God, you can win the
future. So remember those things which will help you forward, but forget
those things which will only hold you back. —Richard C. Woodsome, quoted
in *Inspiring Quotations*, ed. Albert Wells, Jr. (Nashville, TN: Thomas Nelson, 1988),
n.p.

THE SECOND BEST TIME

A greenhouse sign read: "The best time to plant a tree was 25 years ago. The
second best time is today." —Author unknown

132

THE NEW YEAR

A Flower unblown; a Book unread:
A Tree with fruit unharvested:
A path untrod; a House whose rooms
Lack yet the heart's divine perfumes:
A Landscape whose wide border lies
In silent shade 'neath silent skies:
A wondrous Fountain yet unsealed:
This is the Year that for you waits
Beyond Tomorrow's mystic gates. —Horatio Nelson Powers,
Five Thousand Best Modern Illustrations, ed. G.B.F. Hallock
(New York: R. R. Smith, 1931), p. 527.

THE NEW YEAR BEGINS WITH GOD

The beginning of the Bible is the right beginning of time and of all times, "In the beginning God." If we begin with Him, we shall the more easily go on with Him. Taking the first step by His guidance will make it easier for us to take the next, and the next, until we have the habit of walking with Him always. —Robert E. Speer, quoted in *Five Thousand Best Modern Illustrations*, ed. G.B.F. Hallock (New York: R. R. Smith, 1931), p. 527.

THE GIFT OF TIME

Dr. Amos R. Wells said, "Time is a wonderful thing. All men have it, and all have precisely the same amount of it. The gift is given you a little at a time. You must use it at once or it is withdrawn." —G.B.F. Hallock, ed., *Five Thousand Best Modern Illustrations* (New York: R. R. Smith, 1931), p. 535.

Ring out the old, ring in the new, Ring, happy bells, across the snow;
The year is going, let him go; Ring out the false, ring in the true. —Alfred
Lord Tennyson, quoted in *annabelle's Quotation Guide*.
http://www.annabelle.net/topics/newyear.html (accessed December 2000).

Lost time cannot be recaptured. It is lost forever. Therefore, the ticking clock becomes the drumbeat of our lives. We either march to its cadence, or it tramples us. —Elmer Towns

133

ILLUSTRATIONS

ILLUSTRATIONS

A GOOD START

When Booker T. Washington began his school at Tuskegee, classes were held in a vacant chicken coop, and the roof had such a leak that when it rained, a student had to hold an umbrella over Washington's head during his lectures. The college's present success comes from that humble but good start. —G.B.F. Hallock, ed., *Five Thousand Best Modern Illustrations* (New York: R. R. Smith, 1931), p. 536.

PUT SOMETHING BEAUTIFUL INTO EVERY DAY

A college student hung a new wall calendar in her dorm room and declared, "It's going to be a great New Year."

Her roommate asked, "How do you know that? A lot of things could happen this year. A year is a very long time."

She replied, "It will be a beautiful year because I am going to live it one day at a time. And I am going to make sure I put something beautiful into every one of those days." —Elmer Towns

LOOKING FORWARD AND BACKWARD

January is the month of beginnings. Janua in Latin means a door. From it came the name of Janus, ancient Roman god of all beginnings. Janus had two faces so that he might look both forward and back at the same time. He presided over gateways, bridges, doors, and entrances. In his honor, the first month of the year was called January by Pompilius in the seventh century before Christ. —G.B.F. Hallock, ed., *Five Thousand Best Modern Illustrations* (New York: R. R. Smith, 1931), p. 537.

LIVE TODAY

Written on the margins of the Bible John Wesley preached from: "Live today." —G.B.F. Hallock, ed., *Five Thousand Best Modern Illustrations* (New York: R. R. Smith, 1931), p. 536.

A PHILOSOPHY OF LIFE

An elderly man was asked his philosophy of life. He replied:

"Don't work any harder any day than you can recover by sleep at night. Eat simple foods. Exercise and sleep, and take plenty of time for recreation. With the time that is left, make as much money as you can and be content with it. Don't overdraw your nervous capital. Don't overcrowd time." —G.B.F. Hallock, ed., *Five Thousand Best Modern Illustrations* (New York: R. R. Smith, 1931), p. 532.

THE RESOLUTION I CAN KEEP

In the cartoon, *For Better or For Worse*, the family is sitting around the dinner table on New Year's Day making their resolutions.

Mother starts, "I resolve to criticize less and bake more." The family shouts their approval.

Elizabeth adds, "I resolve to take care of the dog, keep my room clean and not fight with my brother."

Father resolves, "I will not lose my temper and I'll fix everything in the house that needs fixing." Mother nods in approval.

Michael announces, "I resolve to ride my bike, hang out with my friends, and watch a lot of TV."

Mother replies, "What kind of a resolution is that?"

Michael says, "The kind I can keep!" —Lynn Johnson, creator of *For Better or For Worse*®

ILLUSTRATIONS

OUGHTTOBIOGRAPHY

A teen sat at the kitchen table on New Year's Eve, writing on a tablet. His mother entered the room, "What are you doing?"

He replied, "I'm writing a list of things I ought to do in the New Year. I'm calling it my *oughttobiography*." —*Saturday Evening Post* (May/June 1999), p. 68.

WHAT'S TIME TO A HOG?

I like the story of the high-pressured, big-city, feed company man that tried to sell a new brand of hog food to a small-time hog farmer. The salesman said, "This feed will make your hogs gain weight at twice the rate of the feed you're using now." The old farmer scratched his head, thought a minute and said, "Aw, what's time to a hog?" —Mark Hollingsworth

135

PASTOR APPRECIATION DAY

Now we ask you, brothers, to respect those who work hard among you, who are over you in the Lord and who admonish you. 1 Thessalonians 5:12

In a survey from the Fuller Institute of Church Growth, research indicates that:

- 80 percent of pastors surveyed felt their ministry affected their family negatively;
- 90 percent felt inadequately trained to cope with job demands;
- 70 percent had a lower self-image than when they started in ministry;
- 70 percent had no one they considered to be a close friend; and
- 50 percent had considered leaving the ministry within the past three months.[1]

While these statistics are sobering, they are a testimony to the deep needs that many American pastors have. The apostle Paul very appropriately exhorted the church of Thessalonica to acknowledge those who ministered to them. Pastor Appreciation Day is a celebration of the work that Jesus Christ is doing through His chosen messengers in the Church today.

In 1992, the nation recognized its first formal Pastor Appreciation Day. Under His Wing Ministries, Inc., organized these first efforts toward recognizing ministers around the United States.[2] Many denominational groups recognize ministers in the month of October—specifically, on the second Sunday of the month.

ILLUSTRATIONS

BE CAREFUL!

The senior pastor visited children's church during Stewardship Month. Wanting to use an object lesson on giving, he picked up the plastic bank that was a replica of a church with a tall steeple. He tripped as he descended the small step to the platform.

A concerned little girl in the front row spoke up, "Be careful, Preacher, our church is in your hands!" —Eric Ritz

THE PASTOR'S NEW CAR

A pastor went to an auto dealer for a new car. He was pleasantly surprised to find out that the dealer had attended his worship service. After a look through the car lot, he spotted a car that caught his eye.

Looking closer, he discovered it had all the desired options. The sticker price wasn't as appealing, however. Announcing his choice to the dealer, he explained that the car was just what he wanted but the price was a little too steep.

"Need I remind you that I'm just a poor preacher?"

The dealer replied, "No, you don't have to remind me, I heard you preach last Sunday!" —Jerry Brecheisen

THE PERFECT PASTOR

The perfect pastor has been found! A computerized survey indicates that he or she

- Preaches 15 minutes or less on Sunday;
- Condemns sin but doesn't expose sinners;
- Works 20 hours per day, and cleans the church on weekends;
- Makes $125 per week, gives $100 to the poor per week and dresses like a millionaire;
- Is 35 years old and has 30 years pastoral experience;
- Loves working with teens, but enjoys working with senior adults even more; and
- Makes 20 pastoral calls a day and is in the office 12 hours each day. —Author unknown

WHAT DOES THE SHEPHERD DO?

On Pastor Appreciation Day, the senior pastor was asked to attend children's church. The children's church teacher wanted him to explain his duties.

The pastor tried to explain that his job was a lot like being a shepherd. "What does the shepherd do for the sheep?" he asked.

One of the students raised a hand, "He skins 'em!" —G.B.F. Hallock, *New Sermon Illustrations for All Occasions* (Westwood, NJ: Fleming H. Revell, 1953), p. 80.

WIRELESS WAND

A little girl brought a friend to church. As the pastor roamed the platform with a wireless microphone, the visiting friend asked, "What's he carrying?"

Her little host said, "I think it's a magic wand. Whenever he talks into it, people go to sleep." —Jerry Brecheisen

CAN YOU TOP THIS?

Three clergymen were having a discussion at the coffee shop.

The Methodist pastor bragged, "One of my ancestors wrote over 200 hymns of the church."

The Baptist minister spoke up, "That's nothing. One of my ancestors pastored the largest church in London."

"Gentlemen," the Jewish rabbi interrupted. "I don't know how to tell you this, but someone in my family wrote the Ten Commandments." —Lowell D. Streiker, comp., *An Encyclopedia of Humor* (Peabody, IL: Hendrickson Publishers, 1998), n.p.

THE ACCOUNTABILITY GROUP

A group of pastors formed an accountability group. At their first meeting in a local restaurant, they began to share their faults.

The first pastor said, "Brothers, I have to confess I'm addicted to late-night TV."

The second pastor responded, "Bless you, brother, I have a need too. I've skipped two church board meetings by calling and saying I was sick when I really wasn't."

The third pastor said nothing.

After a long pause, the other pastors asked compassionately, "Anything you'd like us to pray about, Brother?"

The third pastor nodded, "Yes, I'm afraid so. I have a problem with keeping things in confidence." —Author unknown

ILLUSTRATIONS

IT SOUNDS LIKE A SQUIRREL TO ME

The pastor gathered children from the audience for his children's sermon. "Today, boys and girls, we're going to talk about a creature that lives in the forest."

The children listened intently.

The pastor continued, "Sometimes he lives way up in the air and sometimes he crawls around in the backyard, gathering nuts and carrying them to his treehouse."

"Does anyone here know who I'm talking about?"

A little girl sitting near the pastor grabbed his microphone and announced, "The answer's probably 'Jesus' but it sure does sound like a squirrel to me!" —Elmer Towns

MOWER FOR SALE

A preacher stopped in front of a house where a lawnmower sat in the yard. He needed a lawnmower and noticed the big for-sale sign on the mower.

A junior high boy was sitting by the mower.

"How much for the mower?" The preacher asked.

"$10," the boy replied.

"That's a real bargain," the preacher replied. "Can I give it a start?"

"Go for it," the salesman answered.

He pulled on the starter rope several times, but it just wouldn't start.

"Mister, ya' gotta cuss at it," the boy explained.

The preacher was shocked. "Son, I'm a minister and it's been so long since I cussed, I don't even remember how."

The boy replied, "Keep pullin' that rope, mister, and it'll come back to you."
—David Vaughn

FIFTY YEARS AND THREE EGGS

A young preacher and his wife decided to be more considerate of each other. She promised not to criticize his preaching, and he decided not to look through her dresser drawers anymore.

After 50 years of successful marriage, they gathered with their family for a golden wedding anniversary celebration. Later, as they were putting their gifts away, the preacher noticed an opened dresser drawer. He couldn't resist looking inside. There he found three eggs and $10,000 in cash. "What's this?" he asked, as his wife entered the room.

"Well, you remember I promised to stop criticizing your sermons. Some of them weren't so hot, but instead of making a comment, I put an egg into that drawer as a reminder.

"That's not so bad, fifty years of preaching and only three eggs. But what's all this cash?"

She quietly replied, "Every time I collected a dozen eggs, I sold them."
—Talmadge Johnson

SANCTITY OF LIFE SUNDAY

For you created my inmost being; you knit me together in my mother's womb.
Psalm 139:13

Calvary proves the worth of every life. God so loved the world—from the unborn to the aged. The followers of Christ owe no less than to give their resources to honor the lives of those whom He honored by giving His own life.

On Sanctity of Life Sunday, the Church proclaims its duty to protect life—specifically, the life of the unborn child. Through the last few decades of controversy over abortion, the Church has taken the position to oppose abortion and to uphold the right to life. Christians believe that God is the giver of all life and that all humanity is created in the image and likeness of Him (see Genesis 1:27). The worldly law alone cannot decide the value and dignity of life. Rather, God has expressed His love for each creation. He is the One who is to determine the beginning and end of life.

On this day to celebrate life, many Christians pause to engage in corporate prayer for the unborn children destroyed by abortion. Some also pray for the mothers of the children and the doctors who perform abortions. Many churches encourage peaceful resistance to pro-abortionists, and emphasize speaking the truth in love. Appropriately, other churches offer opportunities for parents of aborted children to receive spiritual and emotional healing through prayer or healing seminars. However the church observes the day, it is appropriate to engage in activities that promote God as the giver of life and wholeness.

140

SERMON SKETCH

CREATED FOR MY GLORY —ELMER TOWNS

TEXT: ISAIAH 43:7

Everyone who is called by my name, whom I created for my glory, whom I formed and made.

A. God is the creator.
B. Man is the creature.
C. Man was created for God's glory.

THE SACREDNESS OF HUMAN LIFE[1]

MAIN TEXT: ECCLESIASTES 3:1,2

There is a time for everything, and a season for every activity under heaven: a time to be born and a time to die, a time to plant and a time to uproot.

A. There is a time to be born.

Before I formed you in the womb I knew you, before you were born I set you apart; I appointed you as a prophet to the nations (Jeremiah 1:5).

B. There is a time to die.

Precious in the sight of the LORD is the death of his saints (Psalm 116:15).

C. Trust the wisdom of God.

"For my thoughts are not your thoughts, neither are your ways my ways," declares the LORD. "As the heavens are higher than the earth, so are my ways higher than your ways and my thoughts than your thoughts" (Isaiah 55:8,9).

Note

1. Stephen Nelson, *The Sacredness of Human Life* (1997).
   http://www.erle.com/Sundays/1997/Sermons/97s-sanctity.html (no access date).

QUOTES

QUOTES

There are two victims in abortion—the child who dies and the mother who bears the emotional and psychological scars. —Stephen Nelson, *The Sacredness of Human Life* (1977). http://www.erle.com/Sundays/1997/Sermons/97s-sanctity.html (no access date).

I am not too small for God's attention. —Author unknown

Life with Jesus is an endless hope, but life without Jesus is a hopeless end. —Author unknown

THANKSGIVING

Therefore, since we are receiving a kingdom that cannot be shaken, let us be thankful, and so worship God acceptably with reverence and awe. Hebrews 12:28

Thanksgiving Day, observed on the fourth Thursday of November in the United States, and on the second Monday of October in Canada, is a secular holiday with sacred significance. From Old Testament festival days to the Last Supper where Jesus offered a prayer of thanksgiving before distributing the elements to His disciples, thanksgiving is a symbol of grateful devotion for God's blessings.

Traced back to the English festivals, Thanksgiving Day has been a national holiday in the United States since 1863. On that fourth Thursday of November, Americans remember with gratefulness the many blessings they have received.

Special attention is drawn to the Pilgrims—the first settlers in what is now the United States. Particularly remembered are the hardships they endured and their subsequent years of blessing. In 1620, the first Pilgrims landed in Massachusetts.[1] Their first years in the New World were difficult—food was scarce and supplies were low. Nearly half of the group died during the first winter. The colonists found shelter in dirt-covered homes. However, an English-speaking Native-American named Squanto came to their aid. Squanto taught the people to plant and harvest crops in the new American climate, and he led the people to a prosperous autumn. With great thankfulness, the Pilgrims called for a thanksgiving feast to celebrate their bounty. The Native Americans were invited to participate, and the feast turned into a weeklong celebration of thanksgiving to God.[2]

Thanksgiving Day is a time when the church can draw the entire community to focus on giving thanks to the Creator of the universe, who has given us "every good and perfect gift" (James 1:17).

143

SERMON SKETCHES

SERMON SKETCHES

TRUE THANKSGIVING —STAN TOLER

MAIN TEXT: COLOSSIANS 3:15

Let the peace of Christ rule in your hearts, since as members of one body you were called to peace. And be thankful.

1. THE BIBLE TEACHES THANKSGIVING

Devote yourselves to prayer, being watchful and thankful (Colossians 4:2).

2. JESUS MODELS THANKFULNESS

At that time Jesus, full of joy through the Holy Spirit, said, "I praise you, Father, Lord of heaven and earth, because you have hidden these things from the wise and learned, and revealed them to little children. Yes, Father, for this was your good pleasure" (Luke 10:21).

A. True thanksgiving comes from the heart.

I love the LORD, for he heard my voice; he heard my cry for mercy (Psalm 116:1).

B. True thanksgiving recognizes God as our source.

How can I repay the LORD for all his goodness to me? (Psalm 116:12).

C. True thanksgiving must be experienced (see Luke 5:26).

3. THE PROBLEM OF INGRATITUDE

But mark this: There will be terrible times in the last days. People will be lovers of themselves, lovers of money, boastful, proud, abusive, disobedient to their parents, ungrateful, unholy (2 Timothy 3:1,2).

4. THE POWER OF THE ATTITUDE OF GRATITUDE

Give thanks in all circumstances, for this is God's will for you in Christ Jesus (1 Thessalonians 5:18).

PAUL'S SECRET TO THANKSGIVING[1]

TEXT: PHILIPPIANS 4:13

I can do everything through him who gives me strength.

A. He believed that God was interested in his life—his circumstances were known to God.
B. He believed that God was sovereign—he believed that God was in control.
C. He believed that God was limitless—he believed that God could do anything, and whatever He did would be in Paul's best interest.

Note

1. Robert Leslie Homes, quoted in *The Abingdon Preaching Annual 1997*, ed. Michael Duduit (Nashville, TN: Abingdon Press, 1996), pp. 22-25.

PAUL'S SECRET TO THANKSGIVING

QUOTES

HYMN

(Written for the 200th anniversary of the Old South Church, Beverly, Massachusetts)

The sea sang sweetly to the shore
Two hundred years ago:
To weary pilgrim-ears it bore
A welcome, deep and low.

They gathered, in the autumn calm.
To their first house of prayer;
And softly rose their Sabbath psalm
On the woodland air.

The ocean took the echo up;
It rang from tree to tree:
And praise, as from an incense-cup.
Poured over earth and sea.

They linger yet upon the breeze,
The hymns our fathers sung:
They rustle in the roadside trees,
And give each leaf a tongue.

The grand old sea is moaning yet
With music's mighty pain:
No chorus has arisen, to fit
Its wondrous anthem-strain.

When human hearts are tuned to Thine,
Whose voice is in the sea,
Life's murmuring waves a song divine
Shall chant, O God, to Thee! —Lucy Larcom, quoted in *Our Holidays In Poetry*, comp. Mildred Harrington and Josephine Thomas (New York: H. W. Wilson, 1950), p. 327.

It is always possible to be thankful for what is given rather than to complain about what is not given. One or the other becomes a habit of life. —Elisabeth Elliot, quoted in *Inspiring Quotations*, ed. Albert Wells, Jr. (Nashville, TN: Thomas Nelson, 1988), p. 200.

Let never day nor night
unhallowed pass,
But still remember what the Lord
hath done. —William Shakespeare, quoted in *Inspiring Quotations*, ed. Albert Wells, Jr. (Nashville, TN: Thomas Nelson, 1988), n.p.

146

No action can be truly complete without gratitude. A symphony without applause at the end isn't a completed symphony. —Peter Stewart, quoted in Yvonne Zipp, "Gratitude and Giving in the 1990s," *The Christian Science Monitor* (November 25, 1998). http://www.csmonitor.com/durable/1998/1/25/fp1-csm.shtml (no access date).

Not what we say about our blessings but how we use them is the true measure of our thanksgiving. —W.T. Purkiser, quoted in *Inspiring Quotations*, ed. Albert Wells, Jr. (Nashville, TN: Thomas Nelson, 1988), n.p.

THANKSGIVING DAY

Brave and high-souled Pilgrims, you who knew no fears,
How your words of thankfulness go ringing down the years;
May we follow after; like you, work and pray,
And with hearts of thankfulness keep Thanksgiving Day. —Annette Wynne, *Our Holidays in Poetry*, comp. Mildred Harrington and Josephine Thomas (New York: H. W. Wilson, 1950), n.p.

We have been a most favored people. We ought to be a most generous people. We have been a most blessed people. We ought to be a most thankful people. —Calvin Coolidge, quoted in *Speaker's Illustrations for Special Days*, ed. Charles L. Wallis (New York: Abingdon Press, 1956), n.p.

Thou who has given so much to me,
Give one thing more—a grateful heart;
Not thankful when it pleaseth me,
As if Thy blessings had spare days,
But such a heart whose pulse
may be Thy praise. —George Herbert, quoted in *Inspiring Quotations*, ed. Albert Wells, Jr. (Nashville, TN: Thomas Nelson, 1988), n.p.

The unthankful heart, like my finger in the sand, discovers no mercies; but let the thankful heart sweep through the day, and as the magnet finds the iron, so it will find, in every hour, some heavenly blessings; only the iron in God's sand is gold! —Henry Ward Beecher, quoted in *Inspiring Quotations*, ed. Albert Wells, Jr. (Nashville, TN: Thomas Nelson, 1988), n.p.

QUOTES

There is no lovelier way to thank God for your sight than by giving a help-ing hand to someone in the dark. —Helen Keller, quoted in *Speaker's Illustrations for Special Days*, ed. Charles L. Wallis (New York: Abingdon Press, 1956), p. 200.

ILLUSTRATIONS

THE THANK-YOU CURE

A psychiatrist had an unusual remedy for neuroses. He called it the "thank-you cure." When a patient came to him showing symptoms of anxiety and fear, the doctor would recommend that for six weeks, whenever anxious thoughts entered the patient's mind, they would think of something they were thankful for and express their gratitude out loud. —Charles L. Wallis, ed., *Speaker's Illustrations for Special Days* (New York: Abingdon Press, 1956), n.p.

THE SPIRITUAL CHAIRLIFT

I rode in the chairlift up Bel-Air Mountains in the Catskills. The valley was clouded over, but as the lift moved up the majestic mountainside, the sun shone more brightly. At the top it shone brilliantly. As I marveled in the view and scanned the vast horizon, I began to give thanks to the Lord. The spirit of thanksgiving is a spiritual chairlift. —Arthur A. Wahmann, quoted in *Speaker's Illustrations for Special Days*, ed. Charles L. Wallis (New York: Abingdon Press, 1956), n.p.

GRATITUDE IN TRAGEDY

A missionary visited the home of one of her national worker colleagues at the news of her brother's death. Entering a tiny room, where the worker and over a dozen other relatives lived, she went to speak to the mother.

Expressing her condolences to the lady who was sitting on a grass mat, she was surprised that the mother suddenly began to express her gratitude. Pointing around the tiny room, the lady began, "Thank you for hiring my daughter. Because of you, we have paint on the wall. You helped to fix the roof that leaked. If you hadn't hired my daughter, we wouldn't have been able to buy screens to keep the mosquitoes out."

The list went on. And the missionary left, humbled by the profound gratitude expressed in a tragic situation. —Faith Finley, "What Have I Thanked God for Today," *Christian Reader* (July/August, 1998), n.p.

149

ILLUSTRATIONS

GOD IS GREAT

An elderly man sat on a folding chair on the porch of a local nursing home with his Bible in his lap. Suddenly he shouted "God is great!"

A ministry intern came over to him and sat in the next chair. "Can't help but hear you talk about God."

"I just read how He parted the waters of the Red Sea and led the Israelites right through," the man said.

"That's right," the intern responded. "I just studied that in Bible School. But did you know that scholars tell us the Red Sea was only about ten inches deep at the time?"

"Well, that makes Him greater than I thought!" the older man shouted.

"What do you mean?" the intern asked.

The elderly man replied, "He not only led those Israelite folk through the Red Sea, He drowned the enemy in less than a foot of water." —Author unknown

A POLITICALLY CORRECT THANKSGIVING

The politically correct fourth grader reported on the origins of Thanksgiving to his class: "The pilgrims came here seeking freedom . . . of you know what. When they landed, they gave thanks to . . . you know who. Because of them, we can worship . . . you know where." —*Leadership Journal*, vol. XIX, no. 4 (Fall 1998), p. 75.

GRATEFULNESS

Mother Theresa told this story in an address to the National Prayer Breakfast in 1994: "One evening we went out, and we picked up four people from the street. And one of them was in a most terrible condition. I told the sisters, 'You take care of the other three; I will take care of the one who looks worst.'

"So I did for her all that my love could do. I put her in bed, and there was such a beautiful smile on her face. She took hold of my hand as she said two words only: "Thank you." Then she died. I could not help but examine my conscience before her. And I asked: *What would I say if I were in her place?* And my answer was very simple. I would have said, 'I am hungry, I am dying, I am in pain' or something similar. But she gave me much more. She gave me her grateful love. And she died with a smile on her face."

Gratitude brings a smile and becomes a gift. —*Leadership Journal*, vol. XV, no. 2 (Spring 1995), p. 48.

THE POOR AND NEEDY

A grandmother took her three-year-old granddaughter to the annual Thanksgiving service. Each family had been instructed to bring food supplies for distribution to the poor and needy in the community. The little granddaughter listened to the instructions and saw the boxes and cans stacked near the platform.

When the Chancel Choir entered the choir loft, the granddaughter suddenly announced loud enough for almost everyone to hear, "Look, Gramma! Here come the poor and needy!" —Cal and Rose Samra, eds., *More Holy Humor* (Nashville, TN: Thomas Nelson, 1997), n.p.

THANKFUL TURKEYS

Two turkeys were reminiscing about their Thanksgiving holidays.

One remarked, "Tell me about your holiday."

The second turkey answered, "I celebrated it the day after Thanksgiving!" —Angela Akers and King Duncan, eds., *Amusing Grace* (Knoxville, TN: Seven Worlds Corporation, 1993), n.p.

THANKSGIVING IN ANY LANGUAGE

"Dad! Guess what?" a junior high student announced. "I can say 'Thanks' in Spanish!"

"That's great!" the father commented. "When are you going to learn it in English?" —Angela Akers and King Duncan, eds., *Amusing Grace* (Knoxville, TN: Seven Worlds Corporation, 1993).

VALENTINE'S DAY

Dear friends, let us love one another, for love comes from God. Everyone who loves has been born of God and knows God. 1 John 4:7

The child of God knows how to love others because of the love he or she has experienced in Christ. That unconditional love is seen directly or indirectly in the expressed sentiments of the season.

While questions exist as to the exact origin of Valentine's Day, the following story is the most generally accepted. Saint Valentine was a Christian priest who lived during the time of the Roman emperor Claudius. Claudius was actively involved in recruiting men for his powerful army. Thinking that unmarried men would be more likely to stay faithful to the Roman military, Claudius ruled that no more marriages could be performed and that all engagements must be canceled.[1]

Valentine found this ruling unfair, and legend tells us that he secretly performed marriage ceremonies for the unfortunate young people. Claudius discovered Valentine's actions, and he threw the priest in jail, where Valentine was beheaded on February 14, 269.[2]

In 496, Pope Gelasius declared February 14 to be a day in honor of St. Valentine.[3] Even before this holiday, February was considered the month to celebrate spring and fertility. The pagan festival of Lupercalia coincided with the Christian Valentine's Day, and scholars are not sure if the two festivals are related or not.[4] In either case, February 14 remains a day that people celebrate romantic and friendly love.

SERMON SKETCH

SWEETHEARTS' SUNDAY

A HEART OF LOVE —STAN TOLER

MAIN TEXT: PROVERBS 4:23

Above all else, guard your heart, for it is the wellspring of life.

A. The heart experiences genuine love.

"Teacher, which is the greatest commandment in the Law?" Jesus replied: 'Love the Lord your God with all your heart and with all your soul and with all your mind.' This is the first and greatest commandment. And the second is like it: 'Love your neighbor as your-self'" (Matthew 22:36-39).

B. The heart expresses heartfelt pain.

For I wrote you out of great distress and anguish of heart and with many tears, not to grieve you but to let you know the depth of my love for you (2 Corinthians 2:4).

C. The heart expresses true generosity.

This service that you perform is not only supplying the needs of God's people but is also overflowing in many expressions of thanks to God (2 Corinthians 9:12).

D. The heart expresses a need for God.

For God is greater than our hearts, and he knows everything. Dear friends, if our hearts do not condemn us, we have confidence before God (1 John 3:20,21).

QUOTES

QUOTES

Let me not to the marriage of true minds
Admit impediments. Love is not love
Which alters when it alteration finds,
Or bends with the remover to remove:
O no! It is an ever-fixed mark
That looks on tempests and is never shaken;
It is the star to every wandering bark,
Whose worth's unknown, although his height be taken.
Love's not Time's fool, though rosy lips and cheeks
Within his bending sickle's compass come:
Love alters not with his brief hours and weeks,
But bears it out even to the edge of doom.
If this be error and upon me proved,
I never writ, nor no man ever loved. —William Shakespeare, *Sonnet CXVI.*
http://albionmich.com/valentine.html (accessed October 29, 1999).

ILLUSTRATIONS

BETTER THAN SALT

A monarch called his three daughters to him. "How much do you love your father?" he asked.

Two of the daughters replied that they loved him more than gold and silver.

"And how about you?" the king said to the third daughter.

She replied, "Father, I love you more than salt."

The answer didn't please the king. "Salt?" he said sharply. "What a strange remark."

The cook of the royal household overhead the remark, and was troubled by the king's response. The next morning, the king's breakfast was prepared without any seasoning. It was bland and tasteless. The king summoned the cook, "Why is my breakfast so tasteless?"

"There is no salt on it, your majesty," the cook replied.

His daughter's words came to mind. The king understood. His daughter loved him so much that nothing was good without him. —Elmer Towns

I WISH TO UNDERSTAND WOMEN

A man is walking along the beach in Hawaii when he finds a lamp. He rubs it and a genie pops out. Thankful for his release, the genie tells the man he will grant him two wishes.

Let's see, the man rubs his chin and thinks out loud, "I'd like a highway back to California because I'm afraid to fly."

Immediately the genie responds, "I'm afraid that is technically impossible, considering the ocean depth and the distance from here to California. Try something else and I promise I will grant you your wish."

"Well then, Mr. Genie, my second wish is to be able to understand women."

The genie slowly shakes his head and replies, "Would you like two lanes or four lanes on that highway?" —Mary Vaughn

ILLUSTRATIONS

THE 50/50 MARRIAGE

A young man saw an elderly couple sitting down to lunch at McDonald's. He noticed that they had ordered one meal and an extra cup. As he watched, the gentleman carefully divided the hamburger in half, then counted out fries, one for her, one for him, until each had half of them. Then he poured half of the soft drink into the extra cup and set it in front of his wife.

The elderly gentleman then began to eat, his wife watching with her hands folded in her lap. The young man decided to ask them if they wouldn't mind if he purchased another meal so they wouldn't have to share. The old man said, "Oh, no. We've been married 50 years and we split everything 50/50."

The young man then asked the wife if she was going to eat her share of the meal and she replied, "Not yet. It's his turn to use the teeth." —Elmer Towns

A CIRCLE GOES ON FOREVER

In the cartoon, *Family Circus*, Billy and Dolly are drawing Valentines. Dolly draws the traditional Valentine heart but Billy opts for a Valentine circle. His explanation, "Instead of a heart I drew a circle. A heart can be broken but a circle goes on forever."
—Bill Keane, *Family Circus*®, King Features Syndicate

TOP 10 THINGS I CAN DO TO BE A BETTER HUSBAND

10. Do something special on our 10th anniversary.
9. Be a better communicator.
8. Be a better listener.
7. Take my wife on more dates.
6. Pray more with my wife.
5. Be a better father.
4. Have other men hold me accountable to being a Christian husband.
3. Meet with other couples for Bible study and support.
2. Treat her like a queen and pray that God will be her King.
1. Be more like Jesus. —Jeffrey Johnson

TOP 10 REASONS WHY I KNOW I'M AN IMPROVING HUSBAND

10. I put my dishes in the sink so she can easily put them into the dishwasher.
9. I let my wife drive the better car even if it isn't low on gas.
8. I almost never tell the children, "Go ask your mother."
7. I can watch TV and pretend I'm listening to a conversation at the same time.
6. I can change a vacuum cleaner belt and bag without a nervous breakdown.
5. I can fold laundry without written instructions.
4. I seek my wife's guidance in important matters such as finding my car keys.
3. I almost never ask my wife to carry my golf clubs.
2. I know how to spell *romance*.
1. I have learned how to salute and say "Yes, Ma'am!" —Jeffrey Johnson

YOU CAN'T BUY LOVE?

According to the International Mass Retail Association, the average person will spend $77.43 per person for Valentine's Day. All told, consumers will spend $1 billion on candy, $1 billion on cards, and $1.6 billion on jewelry. —Susan H. Miller, "Love and Money," *The Indianapolis Star* (February 14, 2000), n.p.

THE FOLDED HANDKERCHIEF

While talking to his wife, Henry pulled out his handkerchief and blew his nose. After several loud snorts, he folded the white handkerchief into a perfect square and put it in his pocket.

His wife quickly responded, "Henry, do you always fold your handkerchief like that?"

"Of course I do," the husband replied. "Been folding it like that for 50 years."

Henry's wife spoke up, "Henry, I don't know how to tell you this, but for 50 years, when I've found your handkerchief neatly folded like that in your pocket, I've just assumed that it was clean and put it back in your dresser drawer."

Henry shook his head, "No wonder I've always had such trouble getting my glasses clean." —Author unknown

ILLUSTRATIONS

157

Section Three

~

CHURCH
CELEBRATIONS

CHOIR CONCERTS

Suddenly a great company of the heavenly host appeared with the angel, praising God and saying, "Glory to God in the highest, and on earth peace to men on whom his favor rests." Luke 2:13,14

The Scriptures are filled with music. From the announcement of the Messiah's birth to His eternal adoration in heaven, faithful voices are pressed into service to proclaim His supreme worthiness. The sound of praise by a solitary servant of Christ is amplified by the dedicated voices of other singers. Together they express, with practice, what the angels expressed with perfection on that night of nights.

Choir concerts fulfill the command in Ephesians 5:19 to "sing and make music in your heart to the Lord." Scripture is full of examples of worship through music. The psalmist writes in Psalm 89:1, "I will sing of the LORD's great love forever; with my mouth I will make Your faithfulness known through all generations." Vocal music is a way to proclaim the attributes of God and to make Him known.

David is probably the best known musician in the Bible; but other singers include Asaph (see Psalms 79—83), the choir that marched along the walls of Jerusalem (see Nehemiah 12:31,38,40), the angels who announced Christ's birth (see Luke 2:8-15) and even Jesus when He sang a hymn with His disciples (see Mark 14:26). Music is a unique form of worship because it is something that springs from the depths of our beings. It has the amazing power to sway emotions. It is, perhaps, one of the deepest means of expression.

In Revelation 5:11-14, we read that many angels, numbering thousands upon thousands, and ten thousand times ten thousand encircle the throne of God and sing. Using loud voices, they declare Christ's crucifixion and the glory that He deserves. How privileged we are to be able to practice the gift of song here on earth.

160

SERMON SKETCH

A WORSHIPING CHURCH —STAN TOLER

MAIN TEXT: JOHN 4:23,24

Yet a time is coming and has now come when the true worshipers will worship the Father in spirit and in truth, for they are the kind of worshipers the Father seeks. God is a Spirit, and his worshipers must worship in spirit and in truth.

Worship is about God, not man. Worship is what He desires from us.

  A. What is real worship?

Praise the Lord, O my soul; and forget not all his benefits (Psalm 103:2).

    1. Worship is the active human response to divine revelation.
    2. Worship is an intentional response of praise, thanksgiving and adoration to God.
    3. Worship is making God first in our lives.
    4. Worship is the reverent devotion, adoration or honor paid to God.

  B. What hinders worship?

They exchanged the truth of God for a lie, and worshiped and served created things rather than the Creator—who is to be forever praised (Romans 1:25).

    1. A critical attitude
    2. An unforgiving spirit
    3. An unfocused mind
    4. Lack of preparation

  C. What are the benefits of true worship?

Let us draw near to God with a sincere heart in full assurance of faith, having our hearts sprinkled to cleanse us from a guilty conscience and having our bodies washed with pure water. Let us hold unswervingly to the hope we profess, for he who promised is faithful (Hebrews 10:22,23).

    1. Joy is for every believer.
    2. Happiness is in serving God.

Jesus answered, "It is written: Worship the Lord your God and serve him only" (Luke 4:8).

ILLUSTRATIONS

YOU MISSED YOUR CALLING

The pastor had a problem. The worship leader had announced his resignation out of frustration over a certain choir member. The choir member, wife of the chairman of the church board, had been the subject of controversy for several years. She couldn't carry a tune!

The pastor called the tone-deaf choir member to his office. For the next thirty minutes, he tried to tactfully ask the lady to drop out of the choir.

"Why should I quit choir?" she asked.

"Well, Sister, I've had over a dozen people tell me that singing in the choir just isn't your calling."

"That's nothing!" the errant alto replied. "I've had two dozen tell me you missed your calling!" —Tracy Sims, *The Christian Index*, vol. 6 (January 28, 1999), p. 10.

SINGING AND THE CIVIL RIGHTS MOVEMENT

Music dominated the background of the civil rights movement. When the marchers marched, they sang. When they sat patiently waiting for a better day, they sang. At the 1963 March in Washington, it was music that moved the bodies, souls, and minds of the people, as Singer Mahalia Jackson prepared the crowd for the memorable speech by Martin Luther King, Jr. —Emerson B. Powery, quoted in the Congress of National Black Churches, Inc. (CNBC), *The African-American Devotional Bible* (Grand Rapids, MI: Zondervan Publishing House, 1997), p. 10.

THE WORSHIP WAR

The preacher and the worship leader were having a feud. Their misunderstanding soon became evident in the worship service.

One Sunday, the preacher preached on commitment. The worship leader closed the service with the song "I Shall Not Be Moved."

The next week, the preacher preached a stirring message about gossip. The worship leader closed with "I Love to Tell the Story."

The tension continued to build, until one night, the preacher announced his resignation. He said, "The Lord is leading me to another place of service."

In response, the worship leader had the congregation stand and sing "Great Is the Lord!" —Elmer Towns

CHURCH ANNIVERSARY

Then Samuel took a stone and set it up between Mizpah and Shen. He named it Ebenezer, saying, "Thus far has the LORD helped us." 1 Samuel 7:12

God delights in supplying the needs of His people. And He also delights in their gratitude for that supply. Thankfulness for God's faithfulness is a strong and noble moment in the life of the local church.

The anniversary of a church is an extremely joyous occasion. Not only is it fitting to celebrate the years a church has served a community, but it is fitting to celebrate the fact that the forces of evil have not been able to defeat God's ministry through the church. All too often, churches today close down—for lack of interest, lack of funding, lack of unity. When a church is able to overcome all of the odds and accomplish effective ministry, there is cause for rejoicing!

At the church anniversary celebration, many pastors will choose to reflect on the church's early days. Older church members may be asked to share about events of long ago. Children may participate in other activities, symbolizing the church's ongoing commitment to the church of the future. The congregation may be asked to engage in an extended period of prayer for the church and its leaders. Ephesians 5:23 tells us that "Christ is the head of the church, his body, of which he is the Savior." This day is certainly a celebration of Christ's leadership. It is a celebration of God's blessing and favor.

ILLUSTRATIONS

ILLUSTRATIONS

WHERE ARE THE LAMPS?

A nobleman built a church for the residents of a tiny village in Europe. Since no one was allowed into the church until its completion, the grateful residents wondered what it would look like.

On the day of dedication, worshipers surveyed their new church.

"Where are the lamps?" one of the members asked.

"There aren't any lamps," the nobleman replied. "There are only hooks on the wall. You must bring your own lamp."

"I'm curious, sir," another member said. "Why must we bring our own lamps?"

The benefactor answered, "It's a reminder that when you are not here, that area of the church will be without light." —Author unknown

WELDED TOGETHER

When I poke a fire, only the tip of the poker need touch the glowing coal, but every atom in the poker is involved, and so is the strength of my arm. It seems to me that we need to follow closely the training that Jesus gave to the disciples. He welded them into a unity as strong as a poker: a poker, we might say, made of very different metals, and welded into an alloy, by His grace and love, stronger than any one metal was before. —Leslie Weatherhead, quoted in *Speaker's Illustrations for Special Days*, ed. Charles L. Wallis (New York: Abingdon Press, 1956), p. 71.

PENTECOST SUNDAY

Peter replied, "Repent and be baptized, every one of you, in the name of Jesus Christ for the forgiveness of your sins. And you will receive the gift of the Holy Spirit. The promise is for you and your children and for all who are far off—for all whom the Lord our God will call." Acts 2:38,39

There is a good deal of interest on the subject of the Holy Spirit. Pentecost is a wonderful time to teach the church family about the importance of the coming of the Holy Spirit to the Church (see Acts 2:1-21).

When the Holy Spirit descended upon the believers at Pentecost, they were strengthened and empowered. Teaching about the Holy Spirit and His work is instrumental in revitalizing the church!

SERMON
SKETCHES

SERMON SKETCH

HE EMPOWERS OUR JOURNEY

MAIN TEXT: JOEL 2:28,29

And afterward, I will pour out my Spirit on all people. Your sons and daughters will prophesy, your old men will dream dreams, your young men will see visions. Even on my servants, both men and women, I will pour out my Spirit in those days.

A. How power was demonstrated in the Old Testament.
   1. Prophecy
   2. National crisis
   3. Divine revelation

B. How power was demonstrated in the New Testament.

Then Peter stood up with the Eleven, raised his voice and addressed the crowd: "Fellow Jews and all of you who live in Jerusalem, let me explain this to you; listen carefully to what I say. These men are not drunk, as you suppose. It's only nine in the morning! No, this is what was spoken by the prophet Joel: 'In the last days, God says, I will pour out my Spirit on all people. Your sons and daughters will prophesy, your young men will see visions, your old men will dream dreams'" (Acts 2:14-17).

   1. The power of signs and wonders
   2. The power of transformation
   3. The power of proclamation
   4. The empowerment of the laity

C. How the Holy Spirit empowers us for the journey.

Even on my servants, both men and women, I will pour out my Spirit in those days, and they will prophesy. I will show wonders in the heaven above and signs on the earth below, blood and fire and billows of smoke. The sun will be turned to darkness and the moon to blood before the coming of the great and glorious day of the Lord. And everyone who calls on the name of the Lord will be saved (Acts 2:18-21).

He empowers us . . .

1. To use our God-given gifts in a powerful ministry to others.
   And you will receive the gift of the Holy Spirit (Acts 2:38).

2. To live the holiness lifestyle in an unholy world.
   The promise is for you and your children (Acts 2:39).

3. To discover spiritual strength and stamina in times of pain and disappointment.
   Save yourselves from this corrupt generation (Acts 2:40).

4. To boldly testify and demonstrate what Joel and Peter preached.
   Those who accepted his message were baptized, and about three thousand were added to their number that day. They devoted themselves to the apostles' teaching and to the fellowship, to the breaking of bread and to prayer (Acts 2:41,42).

QUOTES

QUOTES

We do not need another Pentecost . . . we live in the Age of the Spirit!
—Dr. William Greathouse

The Holy Spirit was given to believers at Pentecost as a deposit on our future inheritance in Christ. —Thomas Hermiz

If the church is to rise to its fullest stature in God, if it is to enjoy the abundant life, if it is to meet all foes in the spirit of triumph, it must rely, not upon its numbers or skills, but upon the power of the Holy Spirit. —Arthur Moore

Pentecost is the center of holiness. Experience the glory of the Spirit's presence among us. —Derl Keefer

168

ILLUSTRATIONS

WHITSUNDAY

The feast of Pentecost came to be called Whitsunday in England. A logical reason (although it may not be historical) is that the term Whitsunday is a contraction of White Sunday. Because of the climate in England, the eve of Pentecost, rather than the eve of Easter, became the time for baptisms (by immersion) because the weather is warmer then. The day was nicknamed for the white robes worn by the candidates for baptism. —William Sydnor, *More than Words*, (New York: Harper & Row Publishers, 1990), n.p.

HE HELPS US SOAR

I was fascinated by a CNN interview with a man who wanted to fly, and inadvertently stopped air traffic near the Los Angeles Airport. He had an innovative idea for flying over his community. Anchoring his lawn chair with a rope, he tied helium-filled balloons to the armrests. He packed a lunch for the flight over his neighborhood and then strapped himself into the chair with a makeshift seat belt. He also included a BB gun to shoot the balloons when he began his descent.

"I cut the anchor ropes loose and expected to go about 1,000 feet in the air, but instead I shot up 11,000 feet!" he exclaimed. Inadvertently he had launched himself into the traffic pattern of the airport, and it took an Air Force helicopter to get him down!

The CNN interviewer's final question: "Sir, were you scared?"

He replied, "Yes, I was, but wonderfully so!"

In a similar way, believers take on the qualities of Christ when filled with the Holy Spirit. When He takes control of our life, we become more buoyant and energized to rise above the circumstances of life. —Stan Toler

NO SUBSTITUTES

In a *Peanuts*® cartoon strip, Lucy looks longingly at Schroeder and screams out, "Guess what? If you don't tell me that you love me, you know what I'm going to do? I'm going to hold my breath until I pass out!"

Schroeder casually looks up from his piano and quietly tells her, "Breath-holding in children is an interesting phenomenon. It could indicate a metabolic disorder. A forty milligram dose of vitamin B6 twice a day might be helpful. I think that's probably it. You need vitamin B6. You might consider eating more bananas, avocados and beef liver." As Schroeder finishes his thought, he returns to his piano playing without missing a beat.

The last frame shows dear Lucy sighing and saying: "I ask for love, and all I get is beef liver!"

Power-packed, Spirit-filled Christians will give the world God's love, not a meaningless substitute! —Derl Keefer

169

REVIVAL

If my people, who are called by my name, will humble themselves and pray and seek my face and turn from their wicked ways, then will I hear from heaven and will forgive their sin and will heal their land. 2 Chronicles 7:14

Clyde Dupin once said, "All great revivals have penetrated the moral and social fabric of our nation." There is tremendous truth in that statement. The need for a world-wide revival is great. Each year churches should plan at least one Revival Sunday to emphasize the importance of the need for spiritual renewal.

SERMON SKETCHES

SERMON
SKETCHES

REVIVAL: OUR GREATEST NEED —ELMER TOWNS

TEXT: PSALM 85:6

Will you not revive us again, that your people may rejoice in you?

A. What is revival?
1. A return to right doctrine
2. A renewal of Christian obedience
3. A willingness to serve others
B. When is revival needed?
1. Church conflict
2. Broken relationships
3. Loss of vision
4. Defeated Christians
C. How is revival achieved?
1. Prayer and fasting
2. Repentance and restitution
3. Generosity in giving
4. Winsomeness in evangelism
D. What are the results of revival?
1. Miracles realized
2. Vision restores
3. Divine healings
4. Church growth

STEPS TO REVIVAL

MAIN TEXT: 1 SAMUEL 7:3

And Samuel said to the whole house of Israel, "If you are returning to the LORD with all your hearts, then rid yourselves of the foreign gods and the Ashtoreths and commit your-selves to the LORD and serve him only, and he will deliver you out of the hand of the Philistines."

Step One: Rid yourselves of the foreign gods (idols).
Step Two: Commit yourself to the Lord.
Step Three: Serve Him only.

171

SERMON
SKETCHES

FASTING FOR SPIRITUAL RENEWAL —STAN TOLER

MAIN TEXT: MATTHEW 6:16-18

A. Examples of fasting
  1. Moses (see Deuteronomy 9:9)
  2. Elijah (see 1 Kings 19:8)
  3. Daniel (see Daniel 10:3)
  4. Jesus (see Luke 4:2)
  5. Paul (see Acts 14:23)

B. Purpose of fasting
  1. To seek help from the Lord
  2. To humble ourselves before the Lord

C. Benefits of fasting
  1. Helps us to rely on God
  2. Helps us to surrender ourselves completely to God
  3. Teaches us discipline

QUOTES

Revival requires holiness in our living! —Don Seymour, quoted in *Revival*, ed. Stan Toler (Cincinnati, OH: CBC Press, 1999), n.p.

Revival brings spiritual power to the powerless. —David Dean, quoted in *Revival*, ed. Stan Toler (Cincinnati, OH: CBC Press, 1999), n.p.

When I fail to fast and pray, I soon lose my spiritual heat and passion for souls. —John Wesley

A revival of religion may be expected when Christians begin to confess their sins to one another. —Charles Finney

Revival is God pouring Himself on His people. For God to pour out Himself, He needs only one person who will unreservedly surrender everything to Him. —Elmer Towns

Revival cannot be worked up; it comes down sovereignly from God when men meet the conditions of God. —Elmer Towns

Hope isn't something we can conjure up as needed. It's the outflow of God's love in our hearts. And if we're without hope, we can ask Him to renew it, just as He revitalized the Holy Spirit's work within us. Without hope, people perish. With God's hope, they believe beyond themselves. —Judith Couchman, *Lord, Have You Forgotten Me?* (Dallas: Word Publishing, 1992), p. 119.

QUOTES

TAKE UP THE CROSS

To be a Christian, one must take up his cross, with all of its difficulties and agonizing and tension-packed content, and carry it until that very cross leaves its mark upon us, and redeems us to that more excellent way which comes through suffering. —Martin Luther King, Jr., in a speech to the National Conference on Religion and Race (1973), quoted in David J. Garrow, *Bearing the Cross: Martin Luther King, Jr., and the Southern Christian Leadership Conference* (New York: Vintage Books, 1988), p. 62.

By a carpenter humankind was made, and only by a carpenter can humankind be remade. —Dennis Kinlaw

Backsliding starts when knee-bending stops. —Albert M. Wells, comp., *Inspiring Quotations,* (Nashville, TN: Thomas Nelson, 1988), n.p.

Do you know what you have to do to backslide? Nothing! —J. Donald Freese, quoted in *Inspiring Quotations,* comp. Albert M. Wells (Nashville, TN: Thomas Nelson, 1988), n.p.

It always seemed absurd to me
To sing of "such a worm as I,"
Until I saw an ugly worm
Become a gorgeous butterfly. —Albert Wells, Jr., ed., *Inspiring Quotations,* (Nashville, TN: Thomas Nelson, 1988), n.p.

ILLUSTRATIONS

I EXPERIENCED CONVERSION

I was saved in a genuine revival. I had prayed for a long time, asking God to be real to me. I prayed the Lord's Prayer sincerely. I asked God to forgive my sins. When I ran out of things to pray, I got in bed but could not go to sleep. Finally, I got on my knees and prayed, "Lord, I've never done it before. Jesus, come into my heart and save me."

Instantly, I experienced conversion and was born again. I had the feeling I had been searching for, but more important, I had inner assurance that I was saved. I cried for joy. I sang "Amazing Grace." I talked to God. I received assurance of my salvation, and to this day, I have never doubted my salvation. —Elmer Towns

SEVEN INDICATIONS OF REVIVAL

1. When the sovereignty of God indicates that revival is near;
2. When wickedness grieves and humbles Christians;
3. When there is a spirit of prayer for revival;
4. When the attention of ministers is directed toward revival;
5. When Christians confess their sins one to another;
6. When Christians are willing to make sacrifices to carry out the new movement of God's Spirit;
7. When ministers and laity are willing for God to promote spiritual awakening by whatever instrument He pleases . . . then revival comes! —Charles Finney

ALL THE KEYS

Lacking power in ministry, the great preacher F.B. Meyer asked a missionary, "Why is God using you and not me?"

The missionary replied, "You must give yourself totally to Jesus."

Later in prayer, Meyer envisioned a ring of keys—the ring of his will and the keys of his life. One key was harder to give, so he decided to keep it.

Jesus asked, "Are all the keys here?"

Meyer replied, "All except one to a tiny closet in my heart."

Jesus said, "If you don't trust me *in* all, don't trust me *at* all."

Sensing that Jesus was receding from him, Meyer finally offered the last key. Jesus took it, cleaned out the secret closet and filled it with so much more.

"What a fool," Meyer thought of his reluctance, "Jesus wanted to take away fake jewels and give me real ones." —Author unknown

REVIVAL

We're in a prerevival state with little pockets springing up, but it's not a full-blown revival yet. If we would confess our sin and repent, perhaps God would ignite the church to be what He wants it to be. —Dale Schlafler, *Promise Keepers*, quoted in Steve Rabey, "Seedbed for Revival," *Christianity Today* (September 1, 1997), p. 4.

THE OBITUARY OF MRS. PRAYER MEETING

Mrs. Prayer Meeting died recently at the First Neglected Church, on Worldly Ave. Born many years ago in the midst of great revivals, she was a strong, healthy child, fed largely on prayers, testimony and Bible study. She had become one of the most influential members of the famous Church family.

For the past several years, Sister Prayer Meeting had been failing in health, suffering stiffness of knees, coldness of heart, inactivity, and weakness of purpose and will power.

Drs. Works, Reform and Joiner had administered large doses of organization, socials, contests and drives but to no avail. An autopsy showed that a deficiency of faith, heartfelt religion and general support contributed to her death.

Survivors include several sobbing saints who mourned her past glory.

In her honor, the church doors will be closed on Wednesday nights. —Author unknown

Section Four

~

FELLOWSHIP AND OUTREACH EVENTS

FRIEND DAY

REACHING OUT TO OTHERS

"Every healthy church wants to improve its outreach efforts. One of the greatest potentials for effective outreach is through reaching friends of the people who already attend your church. Because the friends know and trust those who already come to your church, there is a better possibility that they may attend and respond to the Word of God. Jesus Himself emphasized reaching those within our circle of influence when He recruited His disciples, many of whom were friends or relatives. The recruited disciples then influenced their friends and relatives for Christ.

"There is a right way and a wrong way to get your members to reach their friends for Christ. The quick announcement at the end of a lesson, 'Everyone invite a friend for next week' doesn't usually work because it lacks believability and organization. A planned Friend Day builds credibility and teaches your people biblical evangelism." —Elmer Towns and Stan Toler, *The Year-Round Church Event Book* (Ventura, CA: Gospel Light, 1998), p.110.

SERMON SKETCH

HOW TO WIN AND KEEP FRIENDS —STAN TOLER

MAIN TEXT: JOHN 15:12-14

My command is this: Love each other as I have loved you. Greater love has no one than this, that he lay down his life for his friends. You are my friends if you do what I command.

1. Believe the best in people.
2. Take the initiative.
3. Put others first.
4. Give your best.
5. Be forgiving.

CLOSING HYMN: "WHAT A FRIEND WE HAVE IN JESUS"
(Lyrics by Joseph Scriven and music by Charles C. Converse)

HOW TO WIN YOUR FRIENDS TO CHRIST —STAN TOLER

1. Stay in contact.

    Paul and Timothy, servants of Christ Jesus, To all the saints in Christ Jesus at Philippi, together with the overseers and deacons: Grace and peace to you from God our Father and the Lord Jesus Christ (Philippians 1:1,2).

2. Remember them in prayer.

    I thank my God every time I remember you. In all my prayers for all of you, I always pray with joy because of your partnership in the gospel from the first day until now (Philippians 1:3-5).

3. Keep on encouraging.

    Being confident of this, that he who began a good work in you will carry it on to completion until the day of Christ Jesus (Philippians 1:6).

ILLUSTRATIONS

QUOTES

I came into town and offered them Christ. —John Wesley

Our childhood friends help us cut the psychological umbilical cord that has made us see ourselves through our parent's eyes. Our friends overlook our faults because they are not responsible for us. They show their approval by their acceptance. —Elmer Towns

MY NEIGHBOR
When I was hungry, you gave me food to eat.
When I was thirsty, you gave me water to drink.
When I was homeless, you opened your doors.
When I was naked, you gave me your coat.
When I was weary, you helped me find rest.
When I was anxious, you calmed all my fears.
When I was little, you taught me to read.
When I was lonely, you gave me your love.
When I was in prison, you came to my cell.
When I was on a sick bed, you cared for my needs.
In a strange country, you made me at home.
Seeking employment, you found me a job.
Hurt in a battle, you bound up my wounds.
Searching for kindness, you held out your hand. —Mother Teresa, quoted in James L. Christensen, *Difficult Funeral Services* (Old Tappan, NJ: Fleming H. Revell, 1985), p. 84

ILLUSTRATIONS

FRIENDSHIP KIT

Lifesaver: To remind you of the many times others need your help and, you, theirs.

Cotton ball: For the rough roads ahead, seek the cushioned support of God, your family and friends (see Psalm 18:18).

Rubber band: A reminder to stay flexible.

Sweet and sour candy: To help you appreciate the difference.

Happy face: Smiling not only increases your face value, it's contagious (see Proverbs 15:13).

Candle: To remind you to share your light with others.

Band-aid: For healing hurt feelings—yours or someone elses.

Recipe card: To share a favorite recipe with a friend as a symbol of caring.

Eraser: To remind you that every day you can start with a clean slate. —Author unknown

THE ORDER OF THE MUSTARD SEED

The Order of the Mustard Seed, founded by Count Zinzendorf, had three guiding principles:

* Be kind to all.
* Seek to be good to all.
* Win them all to Christ. —Paul Lee Tan, ed., *Resource* (January/February 1991), p. 43.

FRONTIER TOWN

An old west philosopher was sitting on his porch when a man and his family drove up in a frontier wagon.

"Hey, mister!" the pioneer dad spoke up. "Is this here town friendly?"

"Depends," the philosopher replied. "How was the town where you came from?"

"Not at all friendly!" the pioneer announced. "That's why we left."

The wise old man responded, "Then you'll probably find this town to be the same way."

Later, an almost identical wagon filled with another pioneer family stopped and asked about the friendliness of the frontier town.

"How was it where you came from?" the philosopher asked.

"Friendliest town we ever saw!"

The old man said, "Then you'll probably find this town the same way." —Author unknown

ICE CREAM SOCIALS

SWEET FELLOWSHIP

Fellowship is the number one reason people attend church! With this in mind, what better way to emphasize fellowship than with some good old-fashioned ice cream? An ice cream social can be a wonderful, nonthreatening event for your members to invite their friends and family members to a church gathering.

Lots of good ice cream will encourage fellowship and build good morale!

ILLUSTRATIONS

GOD LIKES HIS ICE CREAM SIMPLE

At one time, I loved chocolate ice cream. Then one day, Mother made some home-made ice cream for my Uncle Herman and Aunt Alice. Chocolate syrup was poured into the stainless steel canister and the dasher—the paddle that swirled the liquid around until it hardened—was put in place. Then the wooden barrel was packed with salt and ice. The little boys churned first because it was easy to turn the handle before the ice cream hardened.

"Don't churn so fast," Uncle Herman chided. "Fast won't get it done any quicker." The longer I churned, the better the chocolate ice cream tasted in my mind.

Soon the handle didn't turn anymore. The ice cream had hardened. Mother unpacked the ice, removed the canister, pulled out the dasher, placed it on a dinner plate, and served it. I began to scoop the homemade ice cream from the dasher.

"Get him a soup bowl!" Uncle Herman said. It might have been one of the passages into manhood—the night I got ice cream in a soup bowl as large as Uncle Herman's bowl.

"That tasted like more," Uncle Herman said with a wink. Soon, more chocolate ice cream was churned. And soon I was consuming another large bowl of chocolate ice cream. "Chocolate—I love chocolate," I exclaimed halfheartedly. I ran around the house to make room for more chocolate ice cream as they churned more.

Thirty minutes later, I was downing another full bowl of chocolate ice cream.

Then came the ice cream headache. It started around my right eye and spread. I began to cry. Mother put a warm cloth on my forehead and my headache went away. About that time, my stomach began to knot. Soon I was doubled over, wailing, "Ooooohhh."

"Want some more ice cream?" Uncle Herman asked. The question hurt as much as my stomachache.

Since that night, I have never again ordered chocolate ice cream. It isn't that I dislike chocolate, but I have learned to love vanilla ice cream more. A deep satisfaction is derived from the simple things in life—the vanilla. God likes His ice cream simple, just like it comes from the cow. —Elmer Towns

NUMBER PLEASE

My brother, Mark, went to an ice cream store. Since there wasn't another customer in the place, he went to the counter and expected fast and courteous service.

Instead of courtesy, he was met with a scolding and some instructions: "You'll have to take a number, and you'll have to wait until your number is called!" —Stan Toler

ILLUSTRATIONS

THE ICE CREAM SALE

On one occasion I arrived at the church to find several families on the church lawn. The ladies' auxiliary was churning ice cream. Previously, I had given a polite lecture to the ladies on not having bake sales to raise funds for missions. They had agreed—and now they were selling ice cream!

"We're not selling it!" the ladies auxiliary president announced on my arrival.

But I noticed they were receiving money for each dish of ice cream. "Then what's going on?" I asked.

"We're raising donations for a gift," she answered.

"A gift for whom?" I asked.

"For our pastor," she replied. I was speechless.

There were dozens of children around the ice cream churn. As I surveyed the churchyard, I thought to myself, *There are more children here than there are in Sunday School; we ought to serve ice cream in Sunday School*—and we did the following Sunday.

Sitting on the front steps of the church for more than an hour, I talked to people attending the ice cream festivity that had never visited the church. I probably had more pastoral contact at the ice cream sale than if I had visited door-to-door.
—Elmer Towns

ROCKY MOUNTAIN ICE CREAM SOCIAL

Celebrate summer the way Rocky Mountain pioneers did, with ice cream, cold beverages, fruit and fun toppings. Here are some ideas, starting with the classic soda fountain favorite, the root beer float:

- **Root Beer Float:** Select a tall glass or mug, and add two scoops of vanilla ice cream. Fill with root beer, and provide both a spoon and a straw.
- **Crimson Cowboy:** Stir a splash of cherry syrup into a glass full of cola.
- **Pike's Peak:** In a tall, wide-mouth glass, stir together a splash of cola with two spoonfuls of chocolate syrup. Add a scoop of vanilla ice cream and stir. Fill the glass with cola to the top.
- **Phosphate:** Add a spoonful or two of cherry syrup to a glass of lemonade. —Lee Recca, "Have an Old-Fashioned Rocky Mountain Ice Cream Social." http://www.sodabrew.com (accessed October 1999).

SUPER BOWL SUNDAY

Super Bowl Sunday is certainly not a religious holiday, but it is indicative of our society's huge interest in sports. The National Football League championship is usually played the last Sunday of January. During the early 1960s there were two major American professional football leagues: the NFL and the American Football League (AFL). The first Super Bowl, held in 1967, was played between the champions of these two leagues. In that game, the Green Bay Packers of the NFL beat the Kansas City Chiefs of the AFL by a score of 35 to 10. However, the championship was not officially called the Super Bowl until 1970, when the two leagues merged to form the modern NFL.[1]

Many churches use Super Bowl Sunday as an outreach event. In keeping with the apostle Paul's goal, "I have become all things to all men so that by all possible means I might save some" (1 Corinthians 9:22), churches have used the event to bring people together for fellowship as well as evangelism.

Some churches set up large screen television monitors and serve refreshments during the game. The game's halftime has become the interval when devotions or videotaped sports testimonials, available from Christian publishers, are presented. Scores of people have made a commitment to Christ through the Super Bowl Sunday events in the local church.

SERMON SKETCH

PRE-GAME PRAYERS —STAN TOLER

TEXT: MATTHEW 26:41

Watch and pray so that you will not fall into temptation. The spirit is willing, but the body is weak.

MESSAGE

Stay alert; be in prayer so you don't wander into temptation without even knowing you're in danger. There is a part of you that is eager, ready for anything in God. But there's another part that's as lazy as an old dog sleeping by the fire.

Did you hear that the 10-minute halftime show at the Super Bowl will cost the NFL about 1.5 million dollars? It's hard for us to comprehend the extravagance associated with what many call the granddaddy of all sports events.

Some Super Bowl Trivia: In 1997, the cost of one second of TV advertising is equivalent to a 30-second ad at the first Super Bowl. The cost of a new car in 1966 was $5,200.00. A new car today costs $18,000.00. If you apply the increase in advertising cost to cars, a new car would cost $96,000. A loaf of bread would cost $6.90. A Pepsi would cost $7.50. And the tithe would be . . .

Have you ever wondered why teams always pray just before the game, but never in practice? Have you ever heard of a team praying in practice?

I don't think we want to point an accusing finger without realizing that we, in fact, may be guilty of praying only before the big games.

For the next few minutes, I want us to think about prayer as preparation.

Jesus is our model. The greatest struggle of his life was the Cross. He prepared Himself and His followers in the Upper Room when He broke the bread and said good-bye. He prepared Himself as He made His way to Gethsemane, where He prayed as His disciples slept. After that prayer time, He faced His arrest and death.

Then he returned to his disciples and found them sleeping. "Could you men not keep watch with me for one hour?" he asked Peter. "Watch and pray so that you will not fall into temptation. The spirit is willing, but the body is weak" (Matthew 26:41).

What we learn from studying Jesus' prayer life is that He was able to pray right before the game because He always prayed in practice.

On the edge of His death, He simply did what He had always done. For Jesus, prayer was preparation for the future.

Matthew understood this when he wrote his Gospel. Jesus prayed at the beginning of His ministry. Prayer would form a vital part of the Sermon on the Mount. When John was arrested and later beheaded, Jesus prayed. When His own troubles began on the Mount of Transfiguration, in the Upper Room, in the Garden and even on the Cross, He prayed.

He was able to face it all because prayer was a golden thread that was stitched into His life from the beginning.

Jesus' words on the eve of His death provide us with help that prayer might become preparation for us too. "Watch and pray so that you will not fall into temptation" (Matthew 26:41).

1. WATCH

The original language has a sense of urgency we do not find in English. "Keep watch with me," He admonished (Matthew 26:38). This word *watch* is sprinkled throughout the New Testament. It was a serious charge for a soldier to be caught sleeping on duty. Hallord Luccok used to say the worst "ism" was not communism, fascism, or secularism, but *somnambulism* (sleepwalking: drowsy, drugged, senses dulled).

The word *watch* also means vigilance. We are encouraged to be alert, ready, with our eyes wide open. Prayer as preparation enables us to watch with vigilance long before the hard times come. Jesus said, "Watch."

2. PRAY

Jesus was able to face his last great difficulties because he had prayed all along. One of the rules of faith is that if we have prayed in practice, it is altogether appropriate to pray before the big events of life.

Illustration

Grandfather was playing with his grandchildren in the wading pool. He lifted his granddaughter up on the slide when chest pains hit him and he went into the house. Shortly after, he settled in his chair, filled with somber thoughts about his chest pains.

His granddaughter (not quite four) opened the patio door and came in. She was naked from playing in the pool, and only had a towel around her shoulders. She took her granddad's hand and said, "Come on, Papa. We need to pray."

"Okay," he said, "But can I pray from here?" "No, Papa. Get down on your knees like this." She knelt down and bowed her head, her hands and fingers together in front of her chin. The towel slipped from her shoulders and lay upon her legs behind her. Papa—followed obediently—kneeling beside his granddaughter.

She prayed, "Dear Jesus God . . ." (She peeked to find her Papa wasn't in the right position to pray, corrected him and continued.) "Dear Jesus God, we don't want Papa's chest to hurt. Please make him better. He's my Papa, Jesus God. Amen."

Papa said, "Amen."

The granddaughter said, "No, Grandpa! You need to say your own prayer!"

Most of us don't need another seminar on prayer. And most of us don't need another book on prayer. Most of us just need to pray our *own* prayers. —From an article appearing in a Wichita Falls, TX, newspaper.

187

SERMON
SKETCHES

3. TEMPTATION

Jesus knew there were temptations, in practice as well as in the big game. He faced the enemy of death because, day after day, He had faced the little temptations of life.

The word "tempt" means trial or test. There in the Garden, he was engaged in the greatest struggle of them all: Your will versus my will—Your way versus my way.

We are tested again and again as Christians. Falling away is the central problem for people of faith in any age. But, Paul wrote to weak, erring, frail Christians in Corinth saying:

No temptation has seized you except what is common to man. And God is faithful; he will not let you be tempted beyond what you can bear. But when you are tempted, he will also provide a way out so that you can stand up under it (1 Corinthians 10:13).

Like us, the disciples learned the hard way about stumbles and falls. But when they put the words of Jesus together, they kept the words of our text. They saw prayer as preparation for all of life and not just before the "big games of life."

And when temptation would come—usually when they least expected it—they would stand firm. They would discover the strangest of truths: despite the leaky roof, despite faulty wiring, despite erratic plumbing, the house of their lives was built on a rock.

They watched and they prayed and even when the temptations came, they stood firm. To pray is to be prepared for whatever life brings.

Illustration

One day Phoebe Palmer came to visit the songwriter, Fanny Crosby. Phoebe sat down at the piano and started to play a melody. She asked Fanny if the melody was saying anything to her. Fanny answered, "It sings to me, 'Blessed assurance Jesus is mine! O what a foretaste of glory divine!'"

In short order, the familiar song, "Blessed Assurance," was finished. The third verse of this great song captures the truth of the lesson:

"Perfect submission, all is at rest. I in my Savior am happy and blest. Watching and waiting, looking above, filled with his goodness, lost in His love."

Is the answer pregame or postgame prayer? I think the answer is "watch and pray" *all* the time!

ILLUSTRATIONS

DEFINITIONS

Draft choice: Selection of a seat near the door

Halftime: The time between the prayer and the offertory

Benchwarmer: Those whose only participation is their attendance on Sunday morning

Quarterback sneak: Parishioners who exit quietly following communion, near the last quarter of service

Fumble: Dropping a hymnal or singing the wrong verse

Backfield in motion: Making two or three trips out during the sermon

Staying in the pocket: What happens to a lot of money that should go to missions

Sudden death: When the preacher goes overtime

Blitz: The stampede to the doors after the service — "Quotes and Comments," *The United Church Observer* (September 1996), p. 55.

NOT IN FRONT OF RESPECTABLE FOLK

With his team trailing by a huge margin, a coach was asked by a TV reporter what he was going to say to his team during half time. He replied, "Sorry, Ma'am, I can't say those kind of things in front of respectable folk." —Cal and Rose Samra, comps., *More Holy Hilarity, Inspirational Humor and Cartoons* (Colorado Springs, CO: WaterBrook Press, 1999), p. 62.

ILLUSTRATIONS

A SUPER HERO

"There's no greater platform than being a quarterback at the Super Bowl." St. Louis Rams quarterback Kurt Warner was answering questions during media day in Atlanta, just days before leading his team in the biggest sports event of the year, and he was using the opportunity to minister for the Lord.

Warner may be the sports story of the millennium. He sat on the bench for four years at Northern Iowa before getting to start as a fifth-year senior. He wasn't drafted by either the NFL or the Canadian Football League. As a free agent, he was cut from the Green Bay Packers, resorting to working evenings as a grocery store stock boy for $5.50 an hour. He played for three years in the Arena Football League, then in NFL Europe last year before the Rams signed him as a third-string backup quarterback.

Last February, he was put on the team's expansion draft list, but was rejected by the new Cleveland Browns. Then, when starter Trent Green was injured in the final exhibition season game, Warner stepped in, threw 41 touchdowns during the season, led the league in a dozen or so categories, was named MVP of the NFL and Miller Lite Player of the Year, and guided his unlikely team to the Super Bowl.

"Kurt Warner is the worst type of quarterback you can play against because you can't scare him," says Warner's teammate, defensive end D'Marco Farr.

"Circumstances don't shake who he is, and circumstances haven't shaped who he is," says Warner's wife, Brenda.

The reasons for Warner's strength lie in his Christian faith and his family—especially his wife and his adopted son, Zachary.

When Warner met Brenda several years ago, she told him she was a struggling, single mom with two children—one of them, Zachary, blind and brain-damaged from a bathtub accident as an infant. She never expected to see Kurt again, but he showed up the next morning to meet the kids with a rose in his hand. It was while playing with Zachary and his Magna Doodle one night that Warner admitted his love for Brenda.

Their relationship grew even stronger when Brenda's parents were killed in a tornado in 1996. Three months later, Kurt became a born-again Christian. Two months after that, he proposed to Brenda.

Warner shares his faith in quiet, powerful ways. He has printed his own football trading cards, featuring the story of the day he turned his life over to Christ, so that he'll have something meaningful to give people who ask for an autograph.

"[My wife] has shown me the best way to respond when you go through struggles," explains Warner. "She's a tremendous inspiration to me."

"And my son is everything to me," he says of Zachary, now 11. "He's the most special child I've ever met. Everything is a struggle for him, but he just keeps going and keeps improving.

"Zachary falls down really hard 10 times a day, but he always gets right back up and exudes pure joy. He touches my life so much.

"For me to throw three interceptions on a football field and get down on myself would be a joke. It gives me a humbling sense of what's important in my life."
—"Pastor's Weekly Briefing," *Focus on the Family* (January 2000), quoted in *USA Today* (January 2000), n.p.

190

Section Five

~

STEWARDSHIP

STEWARDSHIP SUNDAY

Each man should give what he has decided in his heart to give, not reluctantly or under compulsion, for God loves a cheerful giver. 2 Corinthians 9:7

The giving of resources by God's people is a cause for celebration. God loves the generosity of His people. Churches have traditionally treated Stewardship Sunday as a day to celebrate "first fruits" offerings. These offerings can mark the beginning of a particular capital campaign, often to fund a building or renovation program, or they can just present an opportunity to honor God with all our resources. People are encouraged to bring their "first fruits," as mentioned in Exodus 23:19. First fruits represent the best and unspoiled part of one's wealth, and it implies that God is to receive priority in the budget making. He is not to receive one's monetary leftovers but to receive financial priority.

Some churches extend this day of celebration to include more than just financial goals.[1] Some recount the spiritual and financial victories of the past year and make a point of drawing the congregation's attention to God's many blessings. Others use the day as a day of vision casting—to review God's great work through them and to plan together how to continue fulfilling the mission of the church.

Ralph Waldo Beeson once said, "It's the Lord's money. He gave me the gift of making it. I am not smart enough to make that much money on my own. It's His money, and I am going to give it back to Him." True to his word, Beeson gave millions during his lifetime and continues to give to the cause of Christ through his estate.

Stewardship Sunday is valuable because it sets the standard for giving to God on a regular basis. Every church should plan a Stewardship of Life Sunday.

192

SERMON SKETCH

THE PRINCIPLES OF STEWARDSHIP[1]

Jesus reminded the Jewish leaders of several important stewardship principles. The principles apply as much today as they did when Jesus gave the parable.

MAIN TEXT: MATTHEW 21:33-43

Listen to another parable: There was a landowner who planted a vineyard. He put a wall around it, dug a winepress in it and built a watchtower. Then he rented the vineyard to some farmers and went away on a journey. When the harvest time approached, he sent his servants to the tenants to collect the fruit.

The tenants seized his servants; they beat one, killed another, and stoned a third. Then he sent other servants to them, more than the first time, and the tenants treated them the same way. Last of all, he sent his son to them. "They will respect my son," he said.

But when the tenants saw the son, they said to each other, "This is the heir. Come, let's kill him and take his inheritance." So they took him and threw him out of the vineyard and killed him.

Therefore, when the owner of the vineyard comes, what will he do to those tenants?

"He will bring those wretches to a wretched end," they replied, "and he will rent the vineyard to other tenants, who will give him his share of the crop at harvest time."

Jesus said to them, "Have you never read in the Scriptures: 'The stone the builders rejected has become the capstone; the Lord has done this, and it is marvelous in our eyes'?"

Therefore I tell you that the kingdom of God will be taken away from you and given to a people who will produce its fruit.

A. The Principle of Blessing
   1. The landowner saw to it that the vineyard was completely equipped, lacking nothing necessary to run the business of the vineyard efficiently.
   2. Everything in this world belongs to God, who created it and has redeemed it for Himself. A good steward will always manage these resources for the Kingdom's best interests.
B. The Principle of Revelation
   1. When the owner is out of sight, he is usually out of mind. The parable indicates that the landowner committed his vineyard to the workers and went into a far country.
   2. The longer we see the things that God has given us without recognizing His ownership, the more likely we are to begin to see them as our own.
C. The Principle of Belief
   1. The owner of the vineyard had the incredible belief in his employees that they would bring a return on his investment. The owner kept sending people back to collect on his investment.
   2. God loves us so much that even when we hoard or try to keep what belongs to Him, He continues to give us another chance. He is always the God of a second chance.

193

ILLUSTRATIONS

D. The Principle of Judgment
We are not accountable for what we don't have, only for what is committed to us to manage as stewards. A day is coming when every one of us will give an account of our stewardship to God.

Note

1. Stan Toler and Elmer Towns, *Developing a Giving Church* (Kansas City, KS: Beacon Hill Press, 1999), n.p.

194

QUOTES

Each time we write a check it would be wise to remember we are but bankers who manage the Lord's account. —Ron Blue

God has given us two hands—one to receive with and the other to give with. We are not cisterns made for hoarding; we are channels made for sharing. —Billy Graham, quoted in Stan Toler, *Stewardship Starters* (Kansas City, KS: Beacon Hill Press, 1996), n.p.

God gives *to us* what He knows will flow *through us*. —Robert Schuller, quoted in Stan Toler, *Stewardship Starters* (Kansas City, KS: Beacon Hill Press, 1996), n.p.

God demands our tithes and deserves our offerings. —Stephen Olford, quoted in Stan Toler, *Stewardship Starters* (Kansas City, KS: Beacon Hill Press, 1996), n.p.

From what we get, we make a living; what we give, however, makes a life. —Arthur Ashe

Effective resource development is not a money grab. It has a spiritual foundation that makes discipleship its primary goal. The key to resource development is growth in people. —Jay Pankratz, "Growing Generous Givers," *Leadership Journal* (Summer 1998), p. 7. http://www.Christianityonline.com/leadership/813/813090/html (no date accessed).

You can't fake stewardship. Your checkbook reveals all that you really believe about stewardship. A lifestyle could be written from a checkbook. —Ron Blue, quoted in Stan Toler, *Stewardship Starters* (Kansas City, KS: Beacon Hill Press, 1996), n.p.

QUOTES

Tithing is simply an outward expression of spiritual growth, and spiritual growth leads to material growth. —Sir John Templeton, quoted in Stan Toler, *Stewardship Starters* (Kansas City, KS: Beacon Hill Press, 1996), n.p.

Many of us live more for the world that is going than the world that is coming. It takes time, lots of time, to manage all the "things" we accumulate. Time, in the final analysis, is the ultimate resource. —Patrick Morley, *Walking with Christ in the Details of Life* (Nashville, TN: Thomas Nelson Publishers, 1992), p. 40.

Make all you can, save all you can, give all you can. —John Wesley

ILLUSTRATIONS

12 TOOLS FOR CULTIVATING AN UNSELFISH CHURCH

1. Plan ahead.
2. Emphasize discipleship.
3. Bathe in prayer.
4. Identify specific goals.
5. Get commitments.
6. Involve more people.
7. Build trust.
8. Build relationships.
9. Model generosity.
10. Be positive.
11. Spell out sacrifice.
12. Point out the reward. —Jay Pankratz, "Growing Generous Givers," *Leadership \ Journal* (Summer 1998), p. 7. http://www. Christianityonline.com/leadership/813/813090/html (no date accessed).

TREASURE IN THE BACKYARD

The troubles of a young couple escalated. The husband was laid off from his job and then the plumbing in their house went bad.

Digging in the backyard for the water line, they were astonished to uncover a gold coin. That prompted further excavation. Before it was done, their trouble had turned to treasure. They had apparently stumbled on the bounty of some Gold Rush era prospectors and now owned a coin collection of over 1 million dollars. —Elmer Towns

ILLUSTRATIONS

THE BEAUTY OF GIVING

During the American Revolution there lived a Baptist pastor by the name of Peter Miller. He was a man who enjoyed the friendship of George Washington. In the same city lived another man, named Michael Whitman, an ungodly scoundrel who did everything in his power to obstruct and oppose the work of the pastor.

Whitman was involved in an act of treason against the United States. He was arrested and taken to Philadelphia, 70 miles away, to appear before Washington. When the news reached Miller, he walked the 70 miles to Philadelphia to appeal for the life of his enemy.

Admitted to the presence of General Washington, he began to speak for Whitman's life. Washington heard his story through, then said, "No, Peter, I cannot give you the life of your friend." Peter Miller said, "My friend! This man is not my friend. He is the bitterest enemy I have."

Washington said, "You have walked 70 miles through the dust and the heat of the road to appeal for the life of your enemy? Well, that puts this matter in a different light. I will give you, then, the life of your enemy." Miller put his arm around the shoulders of Michael Whitman and led him out of the very shadow of death back to his own home, no longer his enemy but a friend.

When we were enemies, when we were yet without strength, helpless, opposed to God, rebelling again His precepts and principles, leading self-centered lives without regard for His rights, using His goods and His resources, Christ Jesus died for us. That is the beauty of stewardship. That is the beauty of giving. —Stan Toler and Elmer Towns, *Developing a Giving Church* (Kansas City, KS: Beacon Hill Press, 1999), n.p.

A STEWARDSHIP FORMULA

1. Write down the year of your birth.
2. Double it; multiply by 50; add your age.
3. The first four numbers of the answer will be the year you were born, and the last two your age.
4. Now write down your salary.
5. Subtract 90 percent.
6. The balance is the Lord's.
7. Give it to Him, and watch how He will bless the 90 percent. —Author unknown

MILLIONAIRE FOR A DAY

It was a forerunner of a Y2K glitch. A computer error at the local bank accidentally placed over eighty million dollars in one man's account.

He noticed the huge balance when he made an ATM withdrawal. Quickly, he went inside and told the teller he wanted to make sure the balance was correct. She checked his account on the computer and verified the amount.

"I'd like to make a million-dollar withdrawal," he quickly said.

He called his wife and asked her to meet him at the restaurant. There he explained the sudden windfall.

"You know we can't keep this," she remarked.

"I know that," he replied.

He took the check back to the bank. "I know there's been a mistake, but it sure felt good to be a millionaire for a day!" —King Duncan, ed., *Dynamic Illustration* (July/August 1996), n.p.

ILLUSTRATIONS

GIVING IN THE NAME OF THE LORD

A church in Colorado decided to give its Sunday offering to needy residents in a nearby housing complex. Following the service, nearly 500 of its parishioners went door-to-door in the complex and distributed food supplies. "We give you this in the name of the Lord."

They also invited the residents to a lunch that was served in the recreation room of the complex. Many of the residents were in tears. One of the recipients shook the hand of a church member. "I didn't know anyone cared like this." —King Duncan, ed., *Dynamic Illustrations* (September/October 1996), n.p.

I DON'T DO ERRANDS

A beggar stopped by the house of a regular benefactor. "Could you spare a few bucks?" the beggar asked.

Thinking about previous donations to the man, the benefactor replied, "Well, yes I have a few bucks. Hey, what about running to the store for me. I need some groceries."

The beggar answered, "I don't do errands. I just ask for money." —Charles L. Wallis, ed., *Speaker's Illustrations for Special Days* (New York: Abingdon Press, 1956), n.p.

THE SAVIOR IS WATCHING THE OFFERING

To the amazement of his congregation, a well-known pastor accompanied his ushers as they walked the aisles receiving the offering one Sunday.

He later announced from the pulpit, "I have seen your offerings and know what sacrifices you have made or not made. I did this as a reminder that the Savior walks the aisles every Sunday and He sees every cent put into the collection by His people." —William Ward, quoted in *The Evangel* (October 29, 1993), p. 8.

A LESSON IN GIVING

A group of students from a Christian college journeyed to Mexico. Once there, they ministered to families living in cardboard huts near a dump.

Three boys, dirty and shabbily dressed, played near the dump. Through an interpreter, a college student gave one of the boys a single piece of gum.

In a lesson in giving, the boy took the piece of gum, nodded to the student, and tore the gum into three pieces—a piece for each of his friends. —Jim Burns and Greg McKinnon, *Illustrations, Stories and Quotes to Hang Your Message On* (Ventura, CA: Gospel Light, 1997), pp. 165, 166.

PAY WHERE YOU SLEEP

A man built a house across the Arkansas-Missouri line. County officials were confused on how to charge taxes. But the tax law stated that a man must pay taxes according to where he sleeps.

Officials from the state of Arkansas arrived unexpectedly one night in hopes of finding a discrepancy. To their dismay, they looked into the window and saw that the man had positioned his bed directly over the state line. —C. Gordon Bayless, quoted in *Speaker's Illustrations for Special Days*, ed. Charles L. Wallis (New York: Abingdon Press, 1956), n.p.

GIVE IT TO THE CHURCH

A woman called a food distributor with a question about preparing her Thanksgiving Day turkey.

"The turkey has been in the freezer for 10 years, is it safe to eat?"

The operator advised, "It will be all right if the freezer thermostat has been kept near zero degrees." She continued, "However, I'll have to warn you that there is probably a loss of flavor."

"Just what I thought!" the woman replied. "I'll just give it to the church." —Mark Toler-Hollingsworth

I'M THINKING

One of the most celebrated tightwads in history, Jack Benny tells of being approached by a mugger while he was walking down a street.

"Your money or your life," the mugger demanded.

There was a long pause.

"Well?" the robber prodded.

Benny replied, "Don't rush me. I'm thinking! I'm thinking!" —Author unknown

IDEA FOR CHURCH FINANCIAL GROWTH

The church treasurer was lamenting the small amount in the Sunday offering. Talking with the pastor later in the week, he told him he came up with an idea that would add new financial growth to the church. "Pastor, let's petition the government to stop printing one-dollar bills!" —Stan Toler

HERE'S A DOLLAR

An inactive member was approached by a canvasser from the stewardship committee.

He replied, "I don't go to church much, but here's a dollar just to keep me active."

—Charles L. Wallis, ed., *Speaker's Illustrations for Special Days* (New York: Abingdon Press, 1956), p. 16.

DOES GOD DO WINDOWS?

During his message on stewardship, a preacher announced that God promised He would open the windows of heaven for those who tithe.

Later, he was asked about the percentage. "What about five percent?"

"No," the preacher replied, "God doesn't *do* windows for less than 10 percent!" —Stan Toler

WALKING ECONOMY

"I'm a walking economy," a man was overheard to say. "My hairline's in recession, my waist is a victim of inflation, and together they are putting me into a deep depression." —Milton Segal, quoted in Stan Toler, *Stewardship Starters* (Kansas City, KS: Beacon Hill Press, 1996), p. 91.

201

ILLUSTRATIONS

THREE OFFERINGS

A miserly but devout parishioner listened to the announcement of the offering. "There will be three offerings: one for the regular offering, one for the building fund and another for missions."

The miser had forgotten to change the batteries in his hearing aid and so he really didn't understand what the pastor was announcing.

He gave in the first offering.

Astonished, he gave in the second offering.

As the usher handed him the plate for the third offering, he pulled the usher down to him by his tie, "What are you going to do now, frisk me?!" —Author unknown

THE TALKING PARROT

Advised to buy a pet for some companionship, a lonely widow went to a pet store. The store clerk gave her several options but the widow settled on a beautiful parrot. "Does it talk?" the widow asked.

The clerk replied, "Talk? You won't be able to shut it up!"

The widow paid for the bird and took it home with great anticipation.

Two weeks later, the widow called the pet store. "Remember that talking parrot you sold me?"

"Of course," the clerk answered.

"Hasn't said one word!" the widow said in disgust.

The widow was told to come to the store and the clerk sold her some bird supplies. The widow quickly put them in the cage, hoping for a few words from her parrot companion.

First, she installed a little mirror so the parrot would see its reflection and comment. Not a word.

Second, she put a replica of a tree branch in the cage so the parrot could exercise. Not a word.

Third, she put a bell in the cage so the bird could display its musical talents. Not a word.

Calling the pet store again, she said sadly. "My beautiful parrot is dead."

"Dead?" the store clerk exclaimed. "Did it say anything?"

"Yes, finally. As it lay on the bottom of the cage with its feet in the air, it said 'Did you ever think of buying some bird feed for this cage?'" —Elmer Towns

SQUEEZING AN ORANGE DRY

The strong man at the circus concluded his show with a simple but impressive demonstration of his ability to squeeze an orange dry. At the end of his act, he would challenge anyone from the audience to come forward and try to extract, even one drop, from the crushed orange.

On one occasion, a little man, built like Barney Fife, volunteered. Everyone snickered. Undaunted, the little guy stepped onto the stage and took the shriveled-up piece of fruit from the strong man. A hush came over the circus tent as the audience watched in amazement as this small-framed man squeezed out a glass full of orange juice.

After the cheers subsided, the strong man asked the little guy how he did it. Modestly, the little fellow said, "Nothin' to it. I'm the treasurer at the First Church."
—Stan Toler

MONEY TALKS

A father, anxious that his son was losing interest in the church, asked the pastor to have a talk with him.

"Son," the pastor began, "your father is concerned that you're showing little interest in the church. At the very least, I should think you would want to be as interested as he is."

The boy responded, "Have you ever asked him to give $5,000 to the church?"

"Well, no," the pastor answered. "But I know that he gave $500 to the benevolence fund."

"It cost him $5,000 to be a member of the country club. When he gives $5,000 then we'll talk." —Arthur V. Boand, quoted in *Illustrations for Special Days*, ed. Charles L. Wallis (New York: Abingdon Press, 1956), n.p.

THE CHARACTER OF A GROUNDSKEEPER

Part-time groundskeeper for the St. Louis Cardinals, Tim Forneris, responded to a column on why he shouldn't have returned the million dollar baseball hit by Mark McGwire for his 62nd home run.

"I believe som e possessions are priceless. To put an economic value on Mr. McGwire's hard work and dedication is absurd. Being the person who received the ball was a great blessing to me. And being able to return it to Mr. McGwire was a real honor and thrill. I still would not trade that experience for a million dollars."
—Daniel Kadlec, "Personal Time: Your Money," *Time* (February 8, 1999).
http://www.PreachingToday.com (accessed January 30, 2000).

FAILING TO TAKE A RISK

One of the original groups that helped to launch the novel Apple computer, Ronald Wayne sold his 10 percent interest in the company for $800. Getting cold feet and lacking a vision for Apple's future, he failed to take the initial investment risk and focus on the long-term dividend. That $800 investment would be worth more than $300 million today. —*Houston Chronicle*, July 23, 1999, sec. 5F, n.p.

Section Six

SUNDAY
SCHOOL

SUNDAY SCHOOL

SUNDAY SCHOOL CAMPAIGNS

So the word of God spread. The number of disciples in Jerusalem increased rapidly, and a large number of priests became obedient to the faith. Acts 6:7

The first-century church was aflame with enthusiastic growth. People who made the discovery of new life in Christ were anxious for everyone to experience it. Some of that enthusiasm has been dimmed by the cares of time. It needs to be revived, and a Sunday School campaign is a good way to stir the embers.

Sunday School campaigns are not just about numbers. They encourage parishioners to bring their friends and neighbors to church. Psalm 66:5 exhorts us to "Come and see what God has done, [to see] how awesome His works [are] in man's behalf!" Growth campaigns are set aside to tell the community that God is certainly at work in the world, and that His works on our behalf are truly awe-inspiring. They also provide encouragement to parishioners who are timid or who simply neglect to invite others to church. A whole-church effort provides a welcoming atmosphere and fosters a sense of unity in the congregation.

However, the ultimate purpose of Sunday School campaigns is to point people to Jesus Christ. The church has no greater agenda than to share God's Word and pray that loved ones and friends will become "obedient to the faith."

SERMON SKETCHES

A SERVICE OF INSTALLATION OF SUNDAY SCHOOL LEADERS

PRAYER OF THANKSGIVING: SUNDAY SCHOOL SUPERINTENDENT

WORDS OF WELCOME AND STATEMENT OF PURPOSE: PASTOR

INTRODUCTION OF STAFF BY DEPARTMENT: PASTOR

- Children's director and children's teaching staff
- Youth director and youth teaching staff
- Adult director and adult teaching staff
- Support staff: secretary, treasurer, substitute teachers, evangelism director, teaching training director, etc.

SONG: "TELL ME THE OLD, OLD STORY"

(Words and music by Katherine Hankey and William Doane)

SCRIPTURE READINGS: PREACHING AND TEACHING THE WORD

Scriptures from the Living Bible to be read by various teachers.

- Luke 10:16
- 1 Timothy 1:18,19
- 2 Timothy 1:6,7; 2:1,2; 4:1,2.

LITANY OF INSTALLATION: LED BY PASTOR

Leader: Jesus is our model teacher, our example and our guide. He taught by lecture, illustrations, group discussion, visual aids, technology and many other teaching methods.

Staff: May we learn from the Master Teacher.

Leader: Christ, the teacher, showed us that by prayer, study and love people learn.

Staff: May we pray, study and love so that our students may learn.

Leader: The Lord called for participation for those who would learn.

Staff: May we involve our students for their sake.

Leader: The Master teacher gave His all in sacrifice for His students.

Staff: May we sacrifice our time, talent and love for those who would be students of the Word.

Unison: Matthew 28:16-20: "Then the eleven disciples went to Galilee, to the mountain where Jesus had told them to go. When they saw him, they worshiped him; but some doubted. Then Jesus came to them and said, 'All authority in heaven and on earth has been given to me.

Therefore go and make disciples of all nations, baptizing them in the name of the Father and of the Son and of the Holy Spirit, and teaching them to obey everything I have commanded you. And surely I am with you always, to the very end of the age.'"

PRAYER

PRAYER OF INSTALLATION AND COMMISSION: PASTOR

From the start, the Christian church has been a teaching organization. It has been nurtured, sustained, challenged and taught by godly men and women, at times under persecution. It has prepared children for life, encouraged its young people to service, and given a place of service to its adults. In spanning the centuries, Christian education has given knowledge to new converts, wisdom to experienced believers, spared the church from false doctrine, quickened the zeal for evangelism and pricked the conscience of social life. The teaching ministry has prepared Christians for life service, to live life to the fullest, and it has nurtured people to be truly Christian. To this high and noble tradition you have been called and commissioned today. Go and fulfill that important task!

CLOSING PRAYER BY PASTOR

QUOTES

Sunday schools are like sailing ships. If the sails are trimmed properly and the navigation is correct, the ship has a better opportunity to reach its destination. —Elmer Towns, *10 Sunday Schools That Dared to Change* (Ventura, CA: Regal Books, 1993), p. 15.

Though Christian education is a divine task, it is also a process involving humans, a process in which teachers must cooperate with God, rather than work against Him. —Roy B. Zuck, *Spirit-filled Teaching* (Nashville, TN: Word Publishing, 1998), p. 158.

Sunday school is a strategy, not a program. —Rick Warren, quoted in Elmer Towns, *10 Sunday Schools That Dared to Change* (Ventura, CA: Regal Books, 1993), p. 64.

Not only parents and grandparents, but *all* Christians should be concerned with what and how we teach our children. What makes an impact on children is more incense and crosses and leisurely lunches after church than the intricacies of the doctrine of atonement. We should strive for religious infusion as much as for religious instruction. —Lauren F. Winner, Kellet Scholar at Cambridge University

The greatest Sunday school teacher in the world was the man who reached me for Jesus Christ. —Elmer Towns, *10 Sunday Schools That Dared to Change* (Ventura, CA: Regal Books, 1993), p. 10.

ILLUSTRATIONS

CHILD FRIENDLY?

A passerby noticed the remodeling project on the local church. "What are you doing?" he asked the workers.

"Putting up new doors," the worker replied.

"Why is that?" the passerby asked. "The original doors looked great to me."

The worker answered, "They were, but they were too heavy. Only the adults could open them. The pastor said a church doesn't have any right to put up any door that a child can't open." —Roy L. Smith, quoted in *Speaker's Illustrations for Special Days*, ed. Charles L. Wallis (New York: Abingdon Press, 1956), p. 13.

THE SHOULDA SINS

A fifth-grade class had been studying the subject of sin and salvation. On the last Sunday of the study, the teacher reviewed the lessons.

"What is the sin of omission?" she asked. There was a long pause. No answer.

She asked the question again. Same result.

Finally, a hand was raised in the back of the room, "Uh, I think those are the sins we shoulda but didn't." —Cal and Rose Samra, eds., *More Holy Humor* (Nashville, TN: Thomas Nelson, 1997), p. 41.

THE LAWS OF COMMUNICATION

When we pray for God to do things, we should be careful not to ask Him to break the laws by which He runs the universe. Just as it is impossible to communicate from a vacuum, so we should not expect people in our community to attend church services if they don't *know* about the church services. Can we ask God to send people to a church service they don't know about? People are made in the image of God, which means they have intellect, emotion and will (i.e., they have personality). They must:

- *Know* about church meetings;
- *Feel* a reason to attend church meetings; and
- *Decide* to attend church meetings.

Rather than asking God to violate the laws of communication or transcend the laws of communication, we should make use of the laws of communication by marketing and advertising to motivate people to attend our church meetings. —Elmer Towns

IN HEAVEN, GOD IS LIKE YOUR PARENTS

A sixth-grader advised her Sunday school teacher that when you die, God takes care of you just like your parents—except He doesn't holler at you when you don't clean your room. —Dennis R. Fakes, quoted in *More Holy Humor*, ed. Cal and Rose Samra (Nashville, TN: Thomas Nelson, 1997), p. 31.

THE GOOD SAMARITAN

A Sunday school teacher was trying to help her students understand the Good Samaritan story. "Class, what does the story teach us?"

From the back of the room a voice explained, "It means that when you get in trouble, your neighbor ought to help you out." —G.B.F. Hallock, *New Sermon Illustrations for All Occasions* (Westwood, NJ: Fleming H. Revell, 1953), p. 10.

THE FLANNEL BOARD STORIES

A young musician told of being raised in an abusive home. He was invited to attend a small church in the community. Using simple flannel board figures, the Sunday school teacher told stories about Jesus and His love for everyone. The story was new to the young boy but it made him feel loved and safe.

He said that some nights, when the beatings and the yelling started, he would slip out of his house unnoticed and go to the church. Inside, he would lie down near the flannel board. He felt safe there. He learned about true love from the simple stories of his Sunday school teacher. —William Turner, "Mother's Day," *The Abingdon Preaching Annual 1998*, ed. Michael Duduit (Nashville, TN: Abingdon Press, 1997), p. 15.

FREE

A newly established church was successfully reaching families in their community but started to have a problem with parents dropping their children off for church activities and then leaving.

The wise founding pastor solved the problem by sending a note home with the children announcing that a Lassie movie would be shown the following week, and children whose parents did not accompany them would be given a free puppy. —Stan Toler

IT STARTED WITH A SUNDAY SCHOOL TEACHER

When E. Stanley Jones was a teenager, he knelt at the altar during evangelistic services at his church. His Sunday School teacher knelt beside him and began to share God's Word, "For God so loved Stanley, that He gave His only begotten Son, that if Stanley will believe on Him, he shall not perish but have everlasting life."

Still lacking the assurance of his salvation, he returned to the altar the next night. As soon as he knelt, he felt as if heaven had opened on his soul. "I felt like I wanted to put my arms around the whole world and share this."

In later years, E. Stanley Jones did just that. Multitudes were led into the Kingdom because of his missionary endeavors.

And it all started with a Sunday School teacher who was willing to make God's Word personal to a teen. —Author unknown

THE BROTHER AND SISTER COMMANDMENT

The Sunday School teacher was reviewing the lessons on the Ten Commandments with his third-grade class. "What's the commandment that refers to fathers and mothers?"

"Honor thy father and thy mother," a boy on the front row answered.

"Is there a commandment that refers to brothers and sisters?" the teacher followed.

"Yep!" a girl in the back row piped up. "Thou shalt not kill." —Author unknown

THE SUNDAY SCHOOL PICNIC WHIPPIN'

One of my most embarrassing moments as a pastor occurred during my church's Sunday School picnic. Mother suddenly announced to me that I was going to get a spanking.

I was 17 years old, and I pleaded, "Mom, I'm the pastor of the church!"

She answered, "I don't care who you are, you pick on your brother and you're going to get a whippin'!" —Stan Toler

Section Seven

~

DEDICATIONS

COMING OF AGE

When the parents brought in the child Jesus to do for him what the custom of the Law required, Simeon took him in his arms and praised God, saying: "Sovereign Lord, as you have promised, you now dismiss your servant in peace. For my eyes have seen your salvation, which you have prepared in the sight of all people." Luke 2:27-31

Joseph and Mary brought Jesus to the temple to publicly acknowledge what they had both known privately: this child was a special gift from God. His obedient childhood and His future ministry were celebrated in this coming of age ceremony. Those who witnessed the rite were doubly blessed. They were blessed by the devotion of His earthly parents and they were blessed by His adherence to the will of His heavenly Father.

Coming of age ceremonies are strangely neglected in Christian America. Japan, Indonesia, India, and many other countries and religions around the world conduct very significant ceremonies symbolizing an adolescent's emergence into adulthood. For the Christian adolescent, the coming of age ceremony can hold defining spiritual and emotional moments.

In the U.S., these ceremonies are not specific rituals. Instead, parents and child work together to develop an appropriate ceremony. Some families exchange vows outlining new boundaries and new responsibilities. Some children make videotaped statements of their views on various social or spiritual issues.[1]

However a family celebrates, coming of age is a significant part of an adolescent's life. The formality of the event serves to impress upon the mind of the child that he or she has a deeper and more meaningful role to play in history. It is a celebration of a child's future life with God.

QUOTES

Bumper sticker: We have enough youth, what we need is a fountain of smart!
—Author unknown

QUOTES

215

ILLUSTRATIONS

ILLUSTRATIONS

MY GENERATION DROPPED IT

A little boy ran to his mother. "Mom! You know that antique clock of ours that has been passed from one generation to another?"

"Yes," the mother anxiously responded, "what's wrong?"

"My generation just dropped it!" —Robert Leslie Holmes, "The Ultimate Home Security System," *The Abingdon Preaching Annual 1997*, ed., Michael Duduit (Nashville, TN: Abingdon Press, 1996), p. 73.

PISTOL PETE

Legendary basketball player Pete Maravich died at the age of 40. As a boy obsessed with the game, "Pistol Pete" honed his shooting skills throwing a basketball into an imaginary hoop on the ceiling of his room.

Later he set scoring records at Louisiana State University and in the NBA.

One of his fans was TV talk show host Larry King. Hospitalized for heart surgery, King received a letter from Maravich.

"My prayer is that you remain open and God will touch your life as He has mine. When I could not fill my life with basketball, I would simply substitute sex, liquid, drugs or material things. I have finally realized after 40 years that Jesus Christ is in me. He will reveal His truth to you, Larry, because He lives." —Rolf Zettersten, "Pistol Pete Maravich," *Focus on the Family*, no. 21 (1988), p. 14.

COMMISSIONING SERVICE

RECOGNIZING THOSE ENTERING MINISTRY

While they were worshiping the Lord and fasting, the Holy Spirit said, "Set apart for me Barnabas and Saul for the work to which I have called them." So after they had fasted and prayed, they placed their hands on them and sent them off. Acts 13:2,3

The first century Church had a keen sense of teamwork. They knew how much their encouragement meant to their fellow servants. And they knew that acknowledging the gifts and ministries of their fellow believers reflected the Holy Spirit's blessing on their own lives.

Churches hold commissioning services for many different types of activities. Commissioning may be held for missionaries leaving the country, short-term mission trips, the installment of new pastors and lay people entering into new ministry areas, among other things.

In general, commissioning services usually recognize a person or a group of people who are entering into a new field of ministry. A commissioning service serves to inform the congregation and help them to recognize their influential roles as supporters. It also serves to bless the person about to engage in ministry and provide a time to publicly state the person's ministry intentions.

At times, the person being commissioned will take part in reciting vows to service. The congregation will often take part as well, as it recognizes its responsibility to encourage and pray for the new servant. The pastor will usually exhort the people with a passage of Scripture, then close with a prayer of blessing.

217

SERMON SKETCHES

GOD'S STANDARD FOR EFFECTIVE SERVICE —STAN TOLER

MAIN TEXT: 1 CORINTHIANS 4:1-20

1. To be a faithful servant, we must understand our position in the Body of Christ (see vv. 1,2).
2. To be a faithful servant, we must not be sidetracked by criticism (see vv. 3-5).
3. To be a faithful servant, we must recognize what God has given us (see vv. 6-8).
4. To be a faithful servant, we must be sold out for Christ (see vv. 9-13).
5. To be a faithful servant, we must be worthy examples (see vv. 14-17).
6. To be a faithful servant, we must be empowered by God's Holy Spirit (see vv. 18-20).

USED BY GOD —STAN TOLER

1. God uses people who have purpose (Philippians 3:7-14).
2. God uses people who set aside every known hindrance (Hebrews 12:1).
3. God uses people who are consecrated wholly to Him (Romans 12:1).
4. God uses people who know the worth of prayer (James 5:17).
5. God uses people whose eyes are fixed on Jesus (Hebrews 12:2).

MINISTRY: IT'S NOT JUST FOR MINISTERS —STAN TOLER

Whatever you did for one of the least of these brothers of mine, you did for me. Matthew 25:40

1. The foundation of ministry is character (see 1 Timothy 3:1-3).
2. The nature of ministry is service.

Service isn't what takes place at church. It's what happens outside of church. —Derl Keefer

3. The motive of ministry is love.
4. The measure of ministry is sacrifice.
5. The authority of ministry is submission.

If you want to be first, be last; if you want to be greatest, be least; if you want to live, then die. —Elmer Towns

6. The model for ministry is Jesus.

I've laid down a pattern for you. What I've done, you do. I'm only pointing out the obvious. A servant is not ranked above his master; an employee doesn't give orders to the employer. If you understand what I'm telling you, act like it—and live a blessed life (John 13:15-17, THE MESSAGE).

QUOTES

God will not do what people can do; He expects us to do our part. People cannot do what God can do; only God can do His part. —Elmer Towns

The history of Christianity could be written in terms of the ingenious and fatal ways in which Christians have tried to make their faith and practice easy. —David A. MacLennan, quoted in *Speaker's Illustrations for Special Days*, ed. Charles L. Wallis (New York: Abingdon Press, 1956), n.p.

Often, God doesn't call the qualified. But always, He qualifies the called. —Author unknown

If God could not redeem without becoming vulnerable, perhaps there is no other way for us. And thus the question forever faces us: Are we willing to pay the price? —Dennis Kinlaw

How do we prove that we love Christ with undivided love? By giving wholeheartedly free service to the poorest of the poor. We believe it is to Jesus. This thing, if it were not for Jesus, would not be worth doing. —Mother Teresa

Without the spiritual impact of a yielded life, our efforts are relatively futile. With it, our efforts can become marvelously fruitful. —Roy B. Zuck, *Spirit-filled Teaching* (Nashville, TN: Word Publishing, 1998), p. 189.

What God chooses, He cleanses.
What God cleanses, He molds.
What God molds, He fills.
What God fills, He uses. —J. S. Baxter, quoted in *Illustrations for Biblical Preaching*, ed. Michael P. Green (Grand Rapids: Baker Book House, 1989), p. 101.

There are two ways of spreading light: to be the candle, or the mirror that reflects it. —Edith Wharton

219

QUOTES

Character is repeatedly doing the right thing in the right way, in the right attitude, for the right purpose—because it is right. —Elmer Towns

Many look for a large number of people to do the work of God, but a great work for God can be done by one person who is completely dedicated to God. —Elmer Towns

ILLUSTRATIONS

THE SAME IN ANY LANGUAGE

A Christian worker from Argentina was sent to the United States for language training. Eager to tell others about Christ, and unfamiliar with English, his problem was increased by his assignment to a language class comprised mostly of Japanese students.

One day, a Japanese student in the secular school asked him to tell her about Jesus. Soon other Japanese students, many of them Buddhists, gathered around. The Argentinean Christian read from his Spanish/English Bible while the students compared the scripture portions in their Japanese/English Bibles.

A Bible study began that was continued by other Christians. The worker returned to his homeland assured that the Word of God was the same in any language.
—Michael R. Estep, "Bruno," *Herald of Holiness* (March 1997), p. 47.

A CAUSE WORTHY OF SUFFERING

Thoreau was jailed for taking part in a protest. His friend visited him. "What are you doing in jail?" the friend asked.

Thoreau gave a surprising response, "What are you doing out of jail?" —Author unknown

THE MAIL WILL BE DELIVERED

Paul Rader tells the story of a young chaplain stationed on the front lines during the war. Lonely and exhausted, he longed to receive mail from his loved ones.

Before dinner, a jeep arrived with a bag of mail in the back. His name was called and he joyfully opened a stack of letters.

Addressing the mail carrier, he said, "I thought no one cared."

He responded, "Sir, you can be sure that wherever your orders tell you to go, there the mail will be delivered." —Author unknown

THE LORD SENDS IT

Mother Teresa was asked if there was enough money to complete a welfare project. She replied, "Money—I don't think about it. It always comes. The Lord sends it. We do His work. He provides the means. If He does not give us the means that shows He does not want the work." —Kathryn Spink, "Illustrations for Preaching," *The Clergy Journal* (September 1983), p. 21.

ILLUSTRATIONS

SPEAK ABOUT CAREY'S SAVIOR

Cobbler turned missionary, William Carey was a man of great accomplishments. Before his death, he was being considered a missionary hero.

Resisting the lure of missionary fame, his motto was, "The less said about me, the better." And, as he lay dying, he summoned a missionary friend whom he knew would be assisting with his funeral.

He implored, "When I am gone, say nothing about William Carey; speak about Carey's Savior." —Denise George, "Faithfulness Without Fanfare," *Decision* (February 1994), p. 11.

HE DIDN'T LEAVE

Max Lucado writes of the night the disciples caught more fish than they could haul into the boat. In the narrative, Peter reflects on the occasion and of his calling, "I don't know what He saw in me, but He didn't leave. Maybe He thought if I would let Him tell me how to fish, I would let Him tell me how to live." —Max Lucado, *The Greatest Moments* (Nashville, TN: Countryman, 1995), p. 20.

CADILLAC OR CROSS?

A businessman friend drove up in a brand new luxury car. "You look very prosperous these days," I remarked.

"God gave me this Cadillac," he replied. "I believe God wants His people to have the very best of everything."

I said, "You know, that's interesting. God gave you a Cadillac and gave His only begotten Son a cross." —Charles B. Templeton, quoted in *Speaker's Illustrations for Special Days*, ed. Charles L. Wallis (New York: Abingdon Press, 1956), p. 39.

FINISHING THE WORK

Commissioned to find the great missionary David Livingstone, Henry Stanley found him in Africa. Livingstone had not been heard from and his friends and associates were worried. Their worries were well founded. Stanley found Livingstone in very poor health.

As he was caring for the missionary, Stanley expressed his burden for Africa. Together, they explored the regions of that country and shared their concern for its evangelization.

Learning of Dr. Livingstone's death in 1873, Stanley took up the work that Livingstone had left behind. —Author unknown

LITANIES OF DEDICATION

~

A SETTING APART TO GOD

The concept of dedication speaks to us that what we present is to be set apart for something special and in our context to God. We devote a person, plan or thing to God's service. The Greek verb *enkainizo* primarily means "to make new, or renew."[1] As we dedicate whatever we deem necessary, our challenge is to remember that this item is God's and He can do anything He pleases because it is new to Him.

These dedication services are here to serve the busy pastor as a resource to help guide him in the many experiences of worship in which dedication is expected. These dedication services are designed to be used within the worship hour.

A LITANY OF DEDICATION FOR A NEW CHURCH SANCTUARY

~

PRELUDE

CHOIR: "LET US BUILD A HOUSE OF WORSHIP"
(Words and music by Margaret Clarkson and John Zundel)

CALL TO WORSHIP: PSALM 150:1,2,6

Praise the LORD. Praise God in his sanctuary; praise him in his mighty heavens. Praise him for his acts of power; praise him for his surpassing greatness. Let everything that has breath praise the LORD. Praise the LORD.

PASTORAL INVOCATION

LITANY OF DEDICATION

Leader:	Let all the people say "Praise the Lord."
Congregation:	Praise the Lord!
Leader:	Let all the people say "Amen."
Congregation:	Amen.
Leader:	We gather today to praise the Lord who reigns eternally.
Congregation:	For all generations.

Leader:	We gather to dedicate His house of worship for the salvation of humankind.
Congregation:	We dedicate this sanctuary.
Leader:	We covenant together to teach the Holy Scriptures so that coming generations will learn the doctrines of divine truth concerning our God.
Congregation:	We dedicate this sanctuary.
Leader:	We invite the presence of the Holy Spirit into our church.
Congregation:	We dedicate this sanctuary.
Leader:	We invite all to pray for worldwide evangelism that begins here in our community with us telling the good news of the gospel of Jesus Christ.
Congregation:	We dedicate this sanctuary.
All:	In the name of the Father and of the Son and of the Holy Spirit. Amen.

224

A LITANY OF DEDICATION FOR A PLACE OF BUSINESS

~

STATEMENT OF PURPOSE BY PASTOR

Today we have gathered to dedicate this business to the honor and glory of God. (*Name of proprietor*) has asked us to share in this challenging new venture he (she) has undertaken. The outlook is bright with potential as he (she) opens his (her) doors for business. We are here to cheer him (her) on to success. This success is not just for monetary gain but also for the gain of successful characteristics of honesty, fairness, truth and diligence. We congratulate and rejoice with (*name*) for what he (she) has accomplished.

SCRIPTURE READINGS

Deuteronomy 10:12,13; Romans 8:31-39 and 1 Corinthians 3:10-16 read by members of the family or friends.

SPECIAL MUSIC

A WORD OF COMMITMENT BY THE PROPRIETOR

LITANY OF DEDICATION

Leader: Our brother has come to give the keys of his business to you, O God.

Group: We dedicate this business enterprise.

Leader: As each transaction is made, honesty will be the measure of the transaction.

Group: We dedicate this business to You, our Lord.

Leader: We commit this center of business, the staff, the owner and all who serve here to make this business an asset to the community which it services.

PRAYER OF DEDICATION

225

A LITANY OF DEDICATION FOR COMMUNION WARE

~

SCRIPTURE READING: HEBREWS 9:13,14

The blood of goats and bulls and the ashes of a heifer sprinkled on those who are ceremonially unclean sanctify them so that they are outwardly clean. How much more, then, will the blood of Christ, who through the eternal Spirit offered himself unblemished to God, cleanse our consciences from acts that lead to death, so that we may serve the living God!

HYMN OF DEDICATION: "HERE AT THY TABLE, LORD"

(Words and music by May P. Hoyt and William F. Sherwin)

PASTORAL PRAYER OF INVOCATION

LITANY OF DEDICATION

Leader: In holy remembrance of the Jesus who died for us,

People: We dedicate this communion ware.

Leader: Jesus is the why of our celebration of Holy Communion.

People: We dedicate this communion ware of love.

Leader: It is his body and his blood that unites us as His people.

People: We dedicate this communion ware of power.

Leader: We celebrate the testimony of the living presence of Jesus Christ the Son of the living God.

People: We dedicate this communion ware of faith.

Leader: We rejoice at the forgiveness offered to us by the dying Christ as to the thief on the cross.

People: We dedicate this communion ware of peace.

Leader: In fellowship with fellow believers who have been bought with the price of the blood and body of Christ—His Church.

People: We dedicate this communion ware.

SONG: "LET US BREAK BREAD TOGETHER"

THE SERVICE OF COMMUNION

THE LORD'S PRAYER IN UNISON

226

A LITANY OF DEDICATION FOR AMERICAN AND CHRISTIAN FLAGS

OPENING SCRIPTURE: PSALM 33:12

Blessed is the nation whose God is the LORD, the people he chose for his inheritance.

CONGREGATIONAL HYMN: "MY COUNTRY 'TIS OF THEE"

(Words and music by Rev. Samuel F. Smith)

PRESENTATION OF THE COLORS

Local church or community scout troop or veterans organization

PRESENTATION OF THE NEW FLAGS

STATEMENT BY DONOR OR REPRESENTATIVE

ACCEPTANCE OF THE NEW FLAGS BY PASTOR/CHURCH LEADER

THE AMERICAN FLAG

Ask a veteran or current armed force member to share what the flag means to him or her.

HYMN (ALL STANDING): "THE STAR-SPANGLED BANNER"

(Words and music by Francis Scott Key)

SALUTE TO THE AMERICAN FLAG (ALL STANDING)

PLEDGE OF ALLEGIANCE

I pledge allegiance to the flag of the United States of America and to the republic for which it stands, one nation, under God, indivisible, with justice and liberty for all.

CONGREGATIONAL HYMN: "MINE EYES HAVE SEEN THE GLORY"

(Words and music by Mrs. Julia Ward Howe)

THE CHRISTIAN FLAG

Tell the history of the Christian Flag that dates to September 26, 1897.

SALUTE TO THE CHRISTIAN FLAG (ALL STANDING)

PLEDGE TO THE CHRISTIAN FLAG

I pledge allegiance to the Christian flag and to the Savior for whose kingdom it stands; one brotherhood, uniting all true Christians in service and in love.

PRAYER OF DEDICATION

227

A LITANY OF DEDICATION FOR A BAPTISTRY

OPENING REMARKS BY THE MINISTER

The sacrament of baptism continues to be an important part of our Christian heritage. It was John the Baptist who continually called for people to repent and be baptized indicating their forsaking of their old lives of sin to new lives with God. Christ Himself was baptized by John indicating His identification with the human race. Later, as people accepted Christ as Savior and Lord, they were baptized indicating a life changed by God through Christ. As we are baptized, we are identifying with the life, death and resurrection of our Savior Jesus Christ.

SCRIPTURE READING: ROMANS 6:3-13

Or don't you know that all of us who were baptized into Christ Jesus were baptized into his death? We were therefore buried with him through baptism into death in order that, just as Christ was raised from the dead through the glory of the Father, we too may live a new life. If we have been united with him like this in his death, we will certainly also be united with him in his resurrection. For we know that our old self was crucified with him so that the body of sin might be done away with, that we should no longer be slaves to sin—because anyone who has died has been freed from sin. Now if we died with Christ, we believe that we will also live with him. For we know that since Christ was raised from the dead, he cannot die again; death no longer has mastery over him. The death he died, he died to sin once for all; but the life he lives, he lives to God. In the same way, count yourselves dead to sin but alive to God in Christ Jesus. Therefore do not let sin reign in your mortal body so that you obey its evil desires. Do not offer the parts of your body to sin, as instruments of wickedness, but rather offer yourselves to God, as those who have been brought from death to life; and offer the parts of your body to him as instruments of righteousness.

HYMN: "TAKE MY LIFE AND LET IT BE"
(Words and music by Francis R. Havergal)

PRAYER OF DEDICATION OF NEW BAPTISMAL UNIT

BAPTISM OF CANDIDATES BY THE MINISTER

These individuals have accepted Christ as Savior and Lord and have desired to witness to that acceptance by Christian baptism. They are the first to use the new baptistry; however, it is our desire that they are only the beginning of a long line of converts.

CONGREGATIONAL SONG

CLOSING PRAYER

A Litany of Dedication for a Church Instrument

Choir Introit

The Invocation and Lord's Prayer

Statement Concerning the New Instrument by the Pastoral Staff

The Service of Dedication

Leader: That the ministry of music may be enhanced within our church we dedicate this instrument.

People: To the glory of God, the Father of eternal music, that we His people may worship Him, we dedicate this *(name of instrument)*.

Leader: To Christ Jesus, the Savior of the world, where the anthem of praise will sound forth from among us, we dedicate this instrument of glory.

People: We will sing "Holy, Holy, Holy to the Lamb of God."

Leader: To the Holy Spirit whose divine presence inspires our hearts to make melody and harmony in unity we dedicate this instrument of praise.

People: To the fellowship of believers whose gifts have made this day a reality, we dedicate this *(name of instrument)*.

Leader: To all the sacred times of worship that will be solemnized in the music of holiness, we dedicate this instrument of beauty.

All: To those precious moments of meditation and prayer we dedicate this *(name of instrument)* to God the Lord.

Prayer of Dedication by the Senior Pastor

229

DEDICATION OF A CHURCH SIGN

OPENING SCRIPTURE READING: ACTS 2:17-21

"In the last days, God says, I will pour out my Spirit on all people. Your sons and daughters will prophesy, your young men will see visions, your old men will dream dreams. Even on my servants, both men and women, I will pour out my Spirit in those days, and they will prophesy. I will show wonders in the heaven above and signs on the earth below, blood and fire and billows of smoke. The sun will be turned to darkness and the moon to blood before the coming of the great and glorious day of the Lord. And everyone who calls on the name of the Lord will be saved."

People: exalt the name of Jesus as the Body of Christ.
People: We dedicate this sign.
All: We dedicate this sign of love to our Lord and Savior Jesus, the Nazarene, to His church.

HYMN OF DEDICATION

PRAYER OF DEDICATION

SONG OF DEDICATION

RESPONSIVE PRAYER

Leader: The message of the Lord is a sign to all to look to Jesus and live.
People: We dedicate this sign.
Leader: This sign tells our community that we meet here to serve the Lord of lords.
People: We dedicate this sign.
Leader: This sign tells our world that ministry is why we exist.
People: We dedicate this sign.
Leader: This sign tells the times that we gather to glorify and

230

ILLUSTRATIONS

THE LONG-WINDED DEDICATION DAY SPEAKER

A local church wanted to build a new sanctuary. Among the few members was a successful contractor, who agreed to build the sanctuary *absolutely free* if the church met two conditions: They would build it as he saw fit, and they wouldn't allow anyone to enter the building until the day of its dedication.

The board agreed and construction began. Dedication Sunday arrived and the board was thrilled to see inside their new facility. They were alarmed, however, because there was only one row of pews. Then they thought, "What a great idea! Now everyone will have to sit near the front!"

The speaker spoke far too long. The church board fidgeted.

Suddenly, the contractor stood up and walked to the back of the church. He pushed a button on a control panel and to everyone's surprise, the pulpit, along with the long-winded speaker, slowly descended into the basement. —Stan Toler and Elmer Towns, *Developing a Giving Church* (Kansas City, KS: Beacon Hill Press, 1999), n.p.

MOUNTAIN-MOVING MEMBERS

The tiny congregation of a church in the Smoky Mountains received property from an estate. Days before dedicating the new church on the property, the building inspector advised that the parking lot was too small.

They used all of the property for the church construction, and the property was situated at the foothill of a mountain.

They called a prayer meeting that lasted several hours.

The next morning a contractor stopped by. "I'm building a shopping mall down the road," he explained. "And I am in desperate need of fill dirt."

The pastor pointed to the mountain, "We've got plenty of that!"

The contractor continued, "If you'll let me take the dirt from that mountain, I'll top off what's left and make you a parking lot."

Within a few weeks, the contractor had his fill dirt and the "mountain-moving members" had their parking lot. —Larry and Kathy Miller, eds., *God's Vitamin C for the Spirit* (Schenectady, NY: Starburst Publications 1996), p. 55.

HOME DEDICATION

Jonathan Edwards once said, "Every Christian family ought to be as if it were a little church, consecrated to Christ and wholly influenced and governed by His rules."

The dedication of a house is a new found ritual in the life of the Christian community. It is a valuable way to teach our church families the importance of committing everything we have to God!

DEDICATION FOR A CHRISTIAN HOME

LITANY OF DEDICATION

Leader: We have gathered at the new home of *(name)*. As family and friends we have gathered to invoke God's blessings upon this household.

Leader: The foundation of this home rests upon God.

Family (all):   We give our home to You, Lord, from the floor to the ceiling, from wall to wall, to Your purpose and plan.

Leader: As people enter the doors of this home, may they sense the presence of Christ. May this home become a sanctuary of rest from the difficulties of life.

Family (all):   May love decorate every spot in our home.

SCRIPTURE READINGS BY FAMILY MEMBERS

Family member: We commit to the priority of Christ in our home (Luke 10:38-42).

Family member: We commit to the love of God in our home (1 John 4:7-21).

Pastor: May peace be within the halls of this home.

CANDLE CEREMONY

Pastor lights a candle and carries it through the house.

Pastor: May the light of Christ shine forth in the darkness that all may see who dwells here.

Family/Friends: Let old friendships continue and new ones be made in this house.

Family member: "Choose for yourselves this day whom you will serve. . . . But as for me and my household, we will serve the LORD" (Joshua 24:15).

Pastor: We hereby dedicate this house to the glory of God. May the Lord be with you in your going out and your coming in.

SONG: THE DOXOLOGY

PRAYER

A PRAYER

God's mercy spread the sheltering roof,
Let faith make firm the floor;
May friend and stranger, all who come,
Find love within the door.
May peace enfold each sleeping place,
And health surround the board;
From all the lamps that light the halls,
Be radiant joy outpoured.
Let kindness keep the hearth aglow,
And through the windows shine;
Be Christlike living, on the walls,
The pattern and design. —T. L. Paine, quoted in *A Minister's Manual*, ed. Samuel Ward Hutton (Grand Rapids, MI: Baker Book House, 1958), p. 181.

ILLUSTRATIONS

HOME-SWEET-HOME DEDICATION

During the Civil War, union and confederate armies camped near a river in Fredericksburg. During a pause in the terrible fighting, the armies sang their favorite songs—songs that identified their homeland.

Suddenly, the band on the northern side of the river started playing "Home Sweet Home." The armies on both sides stopped their singing and started to cheer. Soon the cheers turned to the singing of the song. It had struck a universal chord that knew no North or South. —John Bardsley, *Clergy Talk* (November 1990), p. 15.

HOME SECURITY SYSTEM

Your home can be protected by the world's ultimate home security system. How? Take God's commands and, "Write them on the doorframes of your houses" (Deuteronomy 6:9). Counteract the terrorism of the times by releasing God's power upon your house. —Robert Leslie Holmes, "The Ultimate Home Security System," *The Abingdon Preaching Annual 1997*, ed. Michael Duduit (Nashville, TN: Abingdon Press, 1996), n.p.

235

INFANT DEDICATION

When the time of their purification according to the Law of Moses had been completed, Joseph and Mary took him to Jerusalem to present him to the Lord. Luke 2:22

The dedication of infants goes all the way back to Old Testament days. Hannah is remembered for praying earnestly for a son. She vowed as she prayed that she "will give [the baby] to the Lord for all the days of his life" (1 Samuel 1:11). When her son Samuel was weaned, Hannah returned to the temple, this time bringing Samuel with her. She presented him to the high priest and thus committed her child to God.

As recorded in the New Testament, Jesus' earthly parents observed the ceremony of dedication. It was a beautiful scene that not only blessed those in attendance, but also was a fulfillment of the prophecy regarding His coming to earth as the Messiah.

Infant dedication is a time for parents to commit their child to God. Like Hannah, parents bring their child to the pastor and publicly declare their commitment to raise their child for the Lord. At the time of dedication, parents are encouraged to pray for their child each day, just as Job did for his children (see Job 1:5). Parents are also encouraged to model the Christian life to their child, and they are exhorted by the minister to discipline their child in love, just as the Lord disciplines us.[1] Finally, the minister may bless the child and pray that he or she will grow up to love the Lord and live for Him, "rooted and established in love, . . . filled to the measure of all the fullness of God" (Ephesians 3:17,19).

A LITANY OF DEDICATION FOR A CHILD

TEXT: MARK 10:13-16

Leader: The task of bringing a child up in our world is complicated and difficult for sensitive, caring parents. It is only through the guiding hand of God along with the inspiration and cooperation of the church that parents receive help. As parents, your words, actions and love will affect *(child's name)* in a multitude of different ways. Your conversations will build his or her mind. Your touch will express the depth of your love for him (her). Your prayers and leadership will be sunlight in his (her) life.

It is from you that *(child's name)* will learn of God. It is your spiritual obligation to receive this child from God's hands. You must teach him (her) to know, experience and love God. You must help his (her) life to unfold as God desires. Your example must include prayer, for it is from you he (she) will learn to pray. Your love for the Word of God will encourage *(child's name)* to learn the truth about Him. Your walk in the fellowship of the church will help *(child's name)* desire to be a part of God's visible body on Earth.

You are to make it your constant effort and prayer to share Jesus with *(child's name)* so that as early as possible *(child's name)* will come to an understanding of salvation and choose on his (her) own to repent, confess and believe the message of Christ and to give himself (herself) in loyal and loving service as a part of the invisible kingdom and visible fellowship of the church.

Do you, Mr. and Mrs. *(name)*, promise before God and this church to pray for and with *(child's name)* so that he (she) will grow in the knowledge of God and in his (her) spiritual life and walk with God?

Parents: We do.

Leader: Do you covenant to train this child in body, mind and spirit for fellowship with Almighty God?

Parents: We do.

QUOTES

QUOTES

BABY

That which makes the home happier,
Love stronger,
Patience greater,
Hands busier,
Nights longer,
Days shorter,
Purses lighter,
Clothes shabbier,
The past forgotten,
The future brighter.
Think not that he is all too young to teach,
His little heart will like a magnet reach
And touch the truth for which you have no speech.
—Froebel, quoted in *The Speaker's Sourcebook*, comp. Eleanor
Doan (Grand Rapids, MI: Zondervan Publishing House, 1960),
n.p.

Children are the anchors that hold a mother to life. —Sophocles, *Phaedra*

It's marvelous how the cry of a little baby in the still of the night evokes
wonder. Usually you wonder which one of you will get up. —Eleanor Doan,
comp., *The Speaker's Sourcebook* (Grand Rapids, MI: Zondervan Publishing House,
1960), n.p.

My deep belief is that all human creatures deserve a happy childhood as a
right and as a prerequisite to normal adulthood, and that the first essential
in happiness is love. —Pearl Buck, quoted in *Speaker's Illustrations for Special
Days*, ed. Charles L. Wallis (New York: Abingdon Press, 1956), n.p.

A baby is the little rivet in the bonds of matrimony. —Eleanor Doan, comp.,
The Speaker's Sourcebook (Grand Rapids, MI: Zondervan Publishing House, 1960),
n.p.

238

Infancy conforms to nobody; all conform to it. —Eleanor Doan, comp., *The Speaker's Sourcebook* (Grand Rapids, MI: Zondervan Publishing House, 1960), n.p.

If it was going to be easy to raise kids, it never would have started with something called "labor." —Angela Akers and King Duncan, eds., *Amusing Grace* (Knoxville, TN: Seven Worlds Corporation, 1993), n.p.

I love these little people; and it is not a slight thing when they, who are so fresh from God, love us. —Charles Dickens, quoted in *Four Thousand Four Hundred Quotations for Christian Communicators*, ed. Carroll E. Simcox (Grand Rapids, MI: Baker Book House, 1991), n.p.

Caption on advertisement for baby product: Yours for a limited time only. —Author unknown

Sign on the church's crib room: "Bawlroom." —Author unknown

BABY SHOES

Often tiny baby feet,
Tired from their play,
Kick off scuffed-up little shoes
At the close of day.
And often tired mothers
Find them lying there,
And over them send up to God
This fervent, whispered prayer:
"God, guide his every footstep
In paths where You have stood;
God, make him brave; God, make him strong;
And please, God, make him good!"
And every man must walk a path,
And every man must choose;
But some forget their mother's prayers
Over their baby shoes. —Mary Homes, "The War Cry," *The Speaker's Sourcebook*, comp. Eleanor Doan (Grand Rapids, MI: Zondervan Publishing House, 1960), n.p.

QUOTES

239

ILLUSTRATIONS

GOD'S SMILING ON ME

A little girl was standing by her parents in the church foyer. Suddenly, she began to twirl around in a sunbeam that shone through the window.

"Look, Mommy!" she said enthusiastically. "God's smiling on me!" —Gwynne M. Day, quoted in *Speaker's Illustrations for Special Days*, ed. Charles L. Wallis (New York: Abingdon Press, 1956), p. 78.

PROVIDING FOR THEIR SAFETY

There is a legend about an ancient ruler who was walking through his kingdom. Stumbling on a sharp stone in the path, he hurt his foot.

Summoning his aides, he commanded, "Cover the face of all the earth with leather and protect my feet."

His aides discussed the impossibility of carrying out the command. One came up with the solution. He presented the monarch with a pair of leather sandals.

Parents cannot cover the world with leather, but they can do their part to make [children] safe by introducing them to Christ. —G.B.F. Hallock, *New Sermon Illustrations for All Occasions* (Westwood, NJ: Fleming H. Revell, 1953), p. 21.

A STRANGER IN THE HOUSE

Newspapers ran the story of a burglar who broke into a house in an upscale neighborhood and lived in the attic for several years before a family member discovered him. The burglar remained quiet when the family was home. When they left, he cooked his meals in the kitchen, watched TV in the family room, and read in the library. The family didn't realize that someone they didn't know was living with them. —Robert Leslie Holmes, "The Ultimate Home Security System," *The Abingdon Preaching Annual 1997*, ed. Michael Duduit (Nashville, TN: Abingdon Press, 1996), p. 13.

END NOTES

Advent
1. *Collier's Encyclopedia*, 1995 ed., s.v. "Advent."
2. Ibid.
3. David G. Truemper, *The World Book Encyclopedia*, 1999 ed., s.v. "Advent."

Easter
1. Mani Niall, "The History of Easter and It's [sic] Custom," online, *Lets Eat*, 1996 http://www.pastrywiz.com/letseat/easter.htm (accessed September 27, 1999).
2. Ibid.
3. Ibid.

Funerals
1. Paul Sheppy, "A Good Funeral," *The Baptist Ministers' Journal* (July 1997), n.p. http://www.pastornet.au/jmm/aasi0037.html (accessed November 1999).
2. Ibid.

Weddings
1. "Wedding Traditions," *USA Bride Internet Wedding Magazine*. http://www.usabride.com/wedplan/a-wed-traditions.html (accessed September 1999).
2. Ibid.
3. Ibid.

Father's Day
1. "History of Father's Day." http://www.bconnex.net/~mbuchana/realms/father/history.html.
2. Ibid.
3. Ibid.

Labor Day
1. "Labor Day," *There's No Place Like Home for the Holidays*. http://www.geocities.com/Athens/Acropolis/1465/laborday.html (accessed September 1999).
2. Ibid.
3. "The Origins of Labor Day." http://www.pbs.org (accessed September 2, 1999).
4. "The History of Labor Day." http://www.dol.gov/dol/opa/public/aboutdol/laborday.html (accessed September 1999).

Mother's Day
1. Holly Hildebrand, "A History of Mother's Day," *Houston Chronicle Interactive*.
2. "History of Mother's Day," *The Realm of Books and Dreams*. http://www.skali.com.my/microsites/skali/events/mday/mday1.html.
3. Hildebrand, "A History of Mother's Day."

241

National Day of Prayer

1. B. A. Robinson, "National Day of Prayer (U.S.)." (May 5, 2000)
2. "National Day of Prayer."
   http://www.forerunner.com/forerunner/X0324NationalDayofPray.html

New Year's Day

1. C. Webber, "New Year's Day," 1998.
   http://www.geocities.com/Heartland/Plains/7214/newyear.html.

Pastor Appreciation Day

1. "Clergy Appreciation Day," *Christianity Online.* http://www.kubik.org/lighter/clergy.htm.
2. Ibid.

Thanksgiving

1. "The Plymouth Thanksgiving Story." http://www.2020tech.com/thanks/temp.html#story.
2. Ibid.

Valentine's Day

1. "Saint Valentine's Day." http://www.pictureframes.co.uk/pages/saintvalentine.html.
2. Ibid.
3. "The History of Valentine's Day," *A & E Television Networks*, 1999. http://www.historychannel.com/exhibits/valentine/history2html.
4. Ibid.

Super Bowl Sunday

1. "Super Bowl," *Microsoft® Encarta® Encyclopedia* 1999. ©1993-1998 Microsoft Corporation.

Stewardship Sunday

1. Paul Hontz, personal interview, December 1, 1999.

Coming of Age

1. "How Do Ethical Societies Celebrate the Coming of Age from Childhood into Young Adulthood?" *Washington Ethical Society*, 1996.
   http://www.ethicalsociety.org/FAQs/answer19.htm

Dedications

1. W.E. Vine, *An Expository Dictionary of New Testament Words* (Grand Rapids, MI: The Zondervan Corporation, 1949), p. 154.

Infant Dedication

1. "Baby Dedication," *Cariboo Road Calvary Chapel.* http://www.calvarychapel.org/caribooroad/believe/babyded.html.

SCRIPTURE REFERENCE INDEX

OLD TESTAMENT

NEW TESTAMENT

MATTHEW

2:1-1112	31
3:1,2,11,15	31, 35
6:9	75
6:16-18	172
10:29-31	59
14:23	123
15:4	75
16:15,16	36
16:16-18	
21:8,9	52
21:33-43	193
22:36-39	153
25:40	218
26:26	45
26:4038	187
26:40,41	186, 187
28:1-10	50
28:16-20	35, 207
28:19	36

MARK

1:4	0034
1:35-37	123
4:34	11
10:13-16	237
11:3-6	52
14:26	160

LUKE

2:8-12	
2:8-15	160
2:13,14	160
2:19	14
2:22	236
2:27-31	214
3:21	123
4:2	172
4:8	161
5	
5:16	122
5:26	144
6:12,13	123
10:16	207

10:21	144
10:38-42	233
22;:19	43
22:31,32	123
23:46	123
24:1	49

JOHN3

1:14	51
1:1-16	15
1:29	51
3:16	15
4:23,24	161
8:12	31
11:35	58
12:12,13	51
13:15-17	218
15:12-14	179
19:16-18	51
19:26,27	105
20:1-18	50
20:21	

ACTS

2:1-21	165
2:14-21,38,39	17, 166
2:17-21	230
2:18-21	167
2:38	34, 167
2:38,39	165
2:389-42	167
4:33	49
6:7	206
13:2,3	217
14:23	172
26:12-16,19,20	128

ROMANS

1:25	161
6:3-13	228
8:31-39	225
12:1	218
13:1-14	92
13:7	85

1 CORINTHIANS

3:10-16	225
3:13-15	97
4:1-20	218
4:18	
9:22	185
10:;1,2	35
10:13	188
10:16,17,18-21	44
10:17	45
11:16	44
11:23-29	44
11:23-33	45
11:26	43

2 CORINTHIANS

2:4	153
5:17	126
9:7	192
11:23-339:12	153

EPHESIANS

2:14	101
3:17,19	236
5:19	160
5:23	163
5:33	66

PHILIPPIANS

1:1-6	179
2:5-11	16
3:7-14	218
4:13	145

COLOSSIANS

3:15	144
3:23	97
4:2	144

1 THESSALONIANS

4:11,12	97
5:12	136
5:18	144

TOPICAL INDEX